SEA MONKEYS

Kris Saknussemm

A MEMORY BOOK

Soft Skull Press
AN IMPRINT OF COUNTERPOINT
Berkeley, California

This is a work of creative nonfiction,
and character names have been changed throughout.

Library of Congress Cataloging-in-Publication Data is available.
ISBN: 978-1-59376-448-7

Cover design by Charles Brock, Faceout Studio
Interior design by Neuwirth and Associates, Inc.

Soft Skull Press
www.softskull.com
An imprint of COUNTERPOINT
1919 Fifth Street
Berkeley, CA 94710

Printed in the United States of America
Distributed by Publishers Group West

10 9 8 7 6 5 4 3 2 1

A Bowlful of Happiness—Instant Pets . . .

On the back page of a Gold Key comic book, I was promised everything I needed.

I was promised a clear acrylic ocean zoo designed like a castle, an aerating ring (whatever that was) and a water purifier. I was promised eggs and a year's food and vitamin supply—even a growth guarantee.

There were so many promises back then. Just add water—*and these longtime favorites of children and the curious come to life before your eyes.*

ACKNOWLEDGMENTS

Portions of this book originally appeared in *The Antioch Review, The Santa Monica Review, New Letters, Witness, Zyzzyva, The Missouri Review, The New England Review, Nimrod, Prairie Schooner, Permafrost, The Fiddlehead, The Chariton Review, The Kansas Quarterly, Gargoyle, Interim, 2Plus2, The Haight Ashbury Literary Journal, The New Mexico Humanities Review, ShatterColors Literary Review, The Nervous Breakdown,* and *The Age Review of Books.*

I am grateful to the Black Mountain Institute of the University of Nevada, Las Vegas, and most especially to Tom E. and Mary Kay Gallagher for their generous support.

I would also like to thank my stepbrother, wherever he may be. He once told me, "The only stories you can really be sure are true are the ones you've forgotten."

I have never forgotten that, and the nature of this book reflects that insight.

SEA MONKEYS

Lights sweep across the walls like the silhouettes of ancient animals in sacred caves.

I'm in my sister's room—where I sleep because of my fear of the dark. Or the almost dark. Or just my fear. The peering eyes in the knots and cracks. The torture chamber in the radiator grate.

One minute you're dragging a duffle bag through wet snow in Brussels—or ripped on tequila listening to the waves in Belize, watching a rib-skinny jaguar sniffing at rotten seaweed.

Then you're suddenly back in your childhood bed listening to the voices in the hall—the floating hallway you never finally find yourself in, only passing through. "Shhh . . ." my sister hisses . . . trying to hear what our parents are arguing about this time. But I only remember ghost words torn from the faded yellow and vacuum tube sparkles of all those bright new tomorrow promised yesterdays . . .

Mutual of Omaha's Wild Kingdom . . . Stand by for Action . . . Janitor in a Drum . . .

The night wind stirs the bearded spruce that dominates our tiny front yard, the blur of branches wrinkling the peppermint-striped curtains, and I close my eyes to the luminous flood . . . like the Huckleberry Hound blue slides our Kenner Give-A-Show Projector casts, which I call our Give-A-Show Protector. Little rainbow windows shot through a plastic ray gun as red as Woody Woodpecker.

Glance over your shoulder, and your stepbrother is right behind you, shooting a daredevil freeway off-ramp on a ten-speed bike late at night. Look back again, and whole dog-eared decades are behind you, and a riderless Triumph motorcycle crosses the Bay Bridge. Wally Gator smears out in green cellophane ectoplasm, becoming Kim Pullman, the fat Mormon with the congenital heart defect. He only wears sweatpants and T-shirts and always smells like butter and damp dishtowels.

Squiddly Diddly and Hokey Wolf fluoresce across the ceiling of a Tudor house looking out at the blinking beacon of Alcatraz, as you step into a cinderblock basement on a hot Michigan summer night, crickets shrill in the crabgrass.

Beyond the punching bags and the hockey sticks is a closet that leads to an attic in Upstate New York—to a lowball parlor in San Jose or a cheap hotel in West Berlin. You cross the creaking planks, leaving footprints in the dust, and emerge on a street in Stratford-upon-Avon just after a freshening rain—where a woman rushing to see Shakespeare's grave has just been run over by a double-decker bus.

Heavens to Murgatroyd. This is the green ghost glow-in-the-dark game where we tumble helplessly toward a fantastic new adventure somewhere along the infinite corridors of time.

"Shhh . . ." my sister whispers. "Pretend you're asleep."

The way the dead do.

TO BEGIN AT THE BEGINNING IS WHERE ALL THE TROUBLE STARTS

SIMULTANEOUS SEA LIONS

Thanks to my grandmother's demented brother Hills (who started off with a nice idea of saving the major world headlines from the day I was born and then became a bit eclectic in his choice of stories), I know some things I might otherwise not.

For instance, on the day I was born, two sea lions that arrived in England for a display in Wellington Pier Gardens managed to escape. A local television personality known as "The Zoo Man" was injured trying to restrain one of the creatures as it "wiggled its way down the pier to freedom."

On the same day in Toledo, Ohio, a sea lion that had escaped from a Canadian zoo was recaptured. According to a report in the *New York Herald Tribune*, officials of the Ontario zoo were going to dispatch a plane to take the animal back, but Toledo Zoo director Phil Skeldon, who helped make the capture in a boathouse on Sandusky Bay off Lake Erie, said he wasn't going to give it up.

"We're going to hold the sea lion," he declared. "We caught it in American waters just like you would a fish, except that it's a mammal, and we consider it ours."

The capture followed an off-and-on chase of several days by Mr. Skeldon and other Toledo Zoo officials. On the previous evening, Mr.

Skeldon was able to slow the mammal down by firing two injections of tranquilizer into its back with a carbon-dioxide-powered dart gun. On the morning of my birthday, fishermen found the sea lion browsing in a boathouse at Sandusky. Mr. Skeldon and Dan Danford, Toledo Zoo's curator of mammals, went to the scene, and Mr. Danford managed to slip a noose over the mammal's head. The men then steered the sea lion to a raft, got it into a cage, and brought it back to Toledo in a station wagon.

So a noose is slipped around the head of one sea lion on the lam, and an umbilical cord is cut, releasing another amphibious mammal into the light. At least I wasn't taken to Toledo in a station wagon. No comets were seen on that, my first official day, but dense, traffic-endangering fog enveloped the city of Melbourne, Australia, a heavy earth shock was recorded in El Salvador and an eighteen-inch section of tailpipe fell from an airplane, narrowly missing seven-year-old Joseph Lamond playing peacefully in his Long Island front yard.

The stock market was up for the third day in a row. Chicago egg futures looked bright. But what of *the* future? I took my first violent breath, and Dr. Rafael Taubenschlag, director of the Warsaw Institute of Papyrology, took his last, killing himself in Krakow at age seventy-seven. Hours later, a famous atomic scientist was found dead of an overdose of sleeping pills in Texas, along with a suicide note he'd written to his wife. "I see no other way out. I cannot bear to go back to the laboratory. So many things undone that I should have done. So many decisions to make that I do not feel capable of making."

Good old Great Uncle Hills. He certainly had an eye for the positive, uplifting stories. Like the fate of the *Cocoa*, one of three jet tanker planes attempting to break the speed record from New York to London, which while taking off from Westover Air Force Base hit high-tension wires and smashed down onto the Massachusetts Turnpike, skidding onto the three-acre farm of Kazimierz Machowski, where its tons of kerosene fuel ignited. Among the fifteen men killed instantly was Norman J. Montellier of New York, age thirty-seven, a UPI writer.

I guess you'd have to say it wasn't a very good day for Polish experts on Egyptian papyruses, atomic scientists or foreign affairs writers from Queens.

You could buy a quart of Astor's All-American Vodka for $4.69 or a new Chrysler for $2,275. In America, the only thing more prevalent than prosperity was Doom—and Doom was big business. In drive-ins across the country, people still gobbled Good & Plenty during the intermission between *The Thing That Couldn't Die* and *The Day the World Ended*, while teenagers faced the shocking facts about grave robbers from outer space. Got your Baby Bee motor airplane or your sun-powered eyeglass hearing aids yet? What's your story about tonight, old Ranger?

While you were watching TV, you could read about Aldo Danesi, who was injured in a freak garage door accident, or the retired Japanese strawberry grower who was killed by a train on his own property in Coyote, California.

Sandra Lee Jennings of Riverside, "a leggy, lovely honey blonde with stars in her big blue eyes," walked off with the Miss California Crown, while a potent chemical known as LSD-25, which quickly releases long-repressed memories and unconscious emotional conflicts, is found to be dramatically helpful in speeding the treatment of mental disease. There's a panel discussion on the wonder drug at the annual American Medical Association meeting, where *Crisada*,

Salvador Dali's 2½-ton, sixty-foot-long artistic contribution, depicts "the caterpillar of man's anxiety contemplating becoming the butterfly of human tranquility."

At the same convention, Dr. Herbert Ratner, public health director of Oak Park, Illinois, laments the widespread breast neuroticism. "Everyone pays lip service to the breasts but the baby," he says. "By default, the subordinate function of the breasts—to add to a woman's beauty and attractiveness—has pre-empted the primary function and has taken on artificial, excessive and idolatrous dimensions."

That night, the live broadcast of eight-year-old Tommy Hunter's open-heart surgery beats out *Cheyenne* in the ratings. The next morning, there are more sightings of sea lions in Lake Erie. Only one gets verified. It proves to be the body of a furniture upholsterer from Vermillion, Ohio, named Fritz Buchenwald.

Mr. Buchenwald's empty boat was later recovered off Marblehead, drifting in the direction of Kelleys Island. An autopsy revealed the cause of death was actually not drowning, although it was clear that the upholsterer had fallen out of his aluminum dinghy. Apparently the man had choked on a sandwich made with Underwood Deviled Ham. A further curious element was that although he was an avid fisherman, it seems he had not taken any of his fishing gear with him. According to Benjamin Cutley, one of his friends, the deceased, who was a widower and had no children, "had looked sort of worried of late, as if he had something important on his mind that he needed to work out."

Perhaps that's what he was trying to do alone out in his boat. Another mystery.

Why does one sea lion wiggle its way down the pier to freedom while another gets drugged, noosed and escorted by administrative officials back to Toledo?

What was so important that Fritz Buchenwald needed to mull over? Had he reached a decision when he reached for that sandwich?

VIEW FROM THE ATTIC

The way my mother tells it, there were weekend trips to her uncle's farm to drink buttermilk and to swat flies. "He was an angry man in suspenders," she mutters. And that's all she ever says.

But her sister let slip once, before one of her six operations, that one Christmas Eve, he swallowed a glass of eggnog and hanged himself from a hay hook while the choir went door to door singing "Good King Wencesias."

The part I really love, though, is that he was discovered by the pretty "mulatto" housekeeper he'd fired suddenly a week before. Imagine. What errand could possibly have drawn her into the hostile shadow of that silo at that exact moment?

We all have our theories. We never speak of them. We never even acknowledge that there are only so many theories to be had. The funny thing to me is that it all seems so clear. I can fool myself into believing I can actually see that moment in the past—the truth of it, I mean. The small-town repertory and the seasons that moved them.

That's why we cling to our family legends. Because they don't tell stories. They *almost* tell stories. They leave us with eggnog and questions, and sometimes, if we're very lucky, an absurd Christmas carol or a second set of footprints, and we go from there.

SAY WHEN

My father lifted me onto his lap as if he intended to tell me one of his growing-up stories. Black Rock Desert, Nevada.

Then he pressed the pedal to the floor—a sudden sound like a man crushing sand between his teeth.

My hands seized the shimmying wheel when he let go, blue air burning by across the vast salt mirror. The arrow trembled to 100, and my mother closed her eyes, singing for him to stop.

But it was a moment in me he was searching for, so there was no stopping—me steering straight for the vanishing lakes—a point in time only I could recognize, having never been there before.

NO SIMPLE SHADOWS

No doubt the mysterious observer is paused in the fringe of shadow for some good reason. Maybe simply not wanting to invade the family portrait. Yet this unidentified interloper distinctly draws the eye away from the four posed people in the central foreground. He's frozen with clenched hands at his side and looks to be somewhere near my father's age, so perhaps he's a buddy or a neighbor. But it's odd the way his upper body and especially his face recedes into shadow, mottling his white T-shirt so that he appears intermittent, his torso intermingling with the light and leaves.

The picture is in black-and-white. The tree is a graceful maple, curiously black, like the space where a tree used to be. In contrast, the family on the bench seems that much brighter. The three from the left are mainly dressed in white. My father, who is perhaps sixteen, wears a white shirt and cuffed dark pants that look comfortable. He's thin of face and lean of body, with dark hair and a high forehead. He has one arm resting on his knee and the other (of course) wrapped around the shoulder of his mother, who years later my sister and I will call Gaja. She has a regrettably large nose and an ill-advised haircut—a wavy flattened bob with shoots out to the side resembling epaulettes. Beside her is my grandfather Karl. He doesn't appear the way I expect, no matter how often I look, even though the maple tree is usually the same.

West Mountain Road in Ridgefield, Connecticut. It's a rundown farm property then, in the early 1940s. I see old fruit trees and a pile of logs and planks behind them. The grass is neat under their feet although it's overgrown in the lot beyond, where there are bee boxes stacked up near a tepee-shaped incinerator. Grandfather Karl looks tense. His face is already lined, two sharp troughs running like scars down his prominent cheekbones. Two other lines run over each eyebrow, as if thumbs have been pressed permanently hard into the skin. Across his forehead is another furrow. It gives his face a worn, wasted cast. He has one shoulder slightly turned and is much wirier than I imagined. Both his oversized hands are entwined in the silky hair of their water spaniel–Irish setter cross that sits between his knees. His expression is frustrated and impatient.

My teenage father (a virgin then), closer than he realizes to war and the Alps of Italy, clings to his mother protectively. She sits solidly between father and son, pleasant, maternally calm. A bastion . . . as she will be later in our family in California.

Aunt Angelou is the fourth occupant of the bench. She has on saddle shoes and white ankle socks and is wearing a rather pretty plaid dress. Her brown hair is shoulder length and she is biting her lip in an awkward smile that looks like she's trying to suppress a giggle. It's somehow obvious in a way that can't quite be identified that there's something not right about her. *Simple* is the word that gets used later.

Another picture. My sister and I are sitting at the drop-leaf table in the Berkeley dining room under the solemn stare of the Japanese woman hanging on the wall as I learn the secrets of transferring to my napkin unwanted portions of carrots and brussels sprouts. Angelou is there with her husband, Dwayne, who is just out of frame. She works as a convalescent hospital nurse (doesn't sound simple to me). Dwayne has something to do with teaching languages for the military but he's really a military historian with family money (rumors of diamond mines and missionaries given over to bad behavior). He's what Gaja calls an odd duck. He speaks like someone important, his deep voice rising out of a cannon-shaped hole where his face should be . . . only the suggestion of a moustache and shining spectacles occasionally glint through the black halo of his baritone. Yet he's strangely devoted to Angelou, taking her on adventures to East Africa and the Congo . . . riding elephants in Thailand . . . Scottish hunting lodges filled with horns and hooves. In one of the pictures of her in the Indonesian archipelago, she stands in tall grass wearing khakis and a pith helmet. Approaching from behind is a Komodo dragon.

In another photograph taken some years later, she's standing proudly holding two glistening rainbow trout beside a camper that looks exactly like the full-sized version of the Tonka truck I received for my sixth Christmas. She's beaming a huge smile and wearing a white cowboy hat just like the one I wore in so many of my childhood pictures, dangling her prize catch from her prosthetic hand.

The picture is a mirror of one of me in Calaveras County one afternoon (the time that Dad and I went to Angels Camp for the Jumping Frog Contest and the Hell's Angels took over the town). I'm sitting in a meadow outside Arnold, in a straw hat with a blue band, the same blue of that Tonka truck, holding up a trout. I look chubby and flushed. Laid out behind me on a rain slicker are ten smallish brown trout (they're chumps, really; Dad should've made me throw them back).

Holding up fish seems to be a family theme. In one photo with my stepbrother Tip, the eastern brook trout are much larger and I'm thinner, more muscular, a humid mist of rain surrounding us, Tip with no shirt despite the moisture, a mass of blackberry bramble and the rusted remains of cars looming behind us on the river's edge.

Tip and I once caught the same fish, standing on different sides of a creek running off the Stanislaus River. If you tried to do it, you couldn't in a million years. We were both hollering, "I got one! I got one!" until we had our lines pulled tight, poles raised and the trout suspended over the water wriggling in the sun. (I later reminded Tip of this incident when he was arrested for grand theft at age eighteen, and he laughed sadly. Following his brain surgery, he said it was one of his childhood memories that remained fixed and bright.)

Then there's the picture of my father fishing Bow River in Alberta. At first glance he looks like himself. It's a honeymoon of sorts—with his third wife Milly. Dad stands on the edge of the slate stone bank wearing his waders, blue shirt, fishing net over one shoulder, creel over the other, his handmade fly rod (the mate of mine) extending out of frame.

His body is cut at the waist by the shadow of a concrete bridge that runs like a frame within the frame. The bridge is smooth, sheer and as white as dried bone, suggesting both light and strength—but also an oppressive weight bearing down on the scene like a tombstone. The water beneath it is black, while the section where Dad is standing is perfectly clear, iridescent with current-softened stones. The stark contrast reminds me of an idea that he often spoke of, cited in Jung and credited to Basil the Great, that the darkness, as in the evil and trouble here on earth, is the shadow cast by heaven.

Below the bridge, the dark water once again opens to the light, a rush of whitewater revealing where the break flow of stones has accumulated. The green world begins too, grass and reeds, saplings and taller pines. Behind the massive white border of the bridge, you can't see any sky, yet the light is intense and whatever shadow Dad casts lies out of frame. I suspect by the fierce quality of the glare that it's late morning or early afternoon and he doesn't have much shadow to cast on either grass or water, which with the immediacy of the bridge and the fact that he's dressed in full fly-casting regalia, tells me that all isn't entirely well. He wouldn't be seriously fly-fishing outside of the early morning or dusk, and he wouldn't have his waders on for fast, shallow water like this. I can see he's using the darkness of the bridge, letting his line drift down where the fish are more likely to be, but ordinarily he'd have strayed farther from such structures, wanting to fish more remote water, wanting to be more to himself. The sum total is that this picture is suspiciously well planned. He's posing for Milly, the new wife, the last chance. He can't straggle upstream the way he used to. And if he could, Milly can't. (She smokes so much she has to be pushed in a wheelchair whenever they go to the airport, even though she'll outlive him by more than twenty years.) Just getting down the bank from the road has probably been the cause of some humor or harsh words, or both. Plus, she doesn't understand fishing. She doesn't grasp the communion with water and time . . . the merging into the past of other pictures where the moments and memories become a river.

This is how my father wants to be seen—in life. And so, with the right kind of haunted camera, you can see that even then, the part of himself that he most admired and valued is going missing, vanishing just like the river that seems to flow through him into the black rectangle of bridge shadow. Perpetual fisherman. His pole points like a lecturer's baton to something out of reach, out of frame.

Angelou's husband Dwayne wears safari suits, speaks Russian and seems to exude firearms, to my mother's horror. Revolvers, hunting rifles. He quotes Jack London speaking about the cold and the quiet of the Klondike: "You get your perspective; I got mine." Over chicken Maryland and molded cranberry salad, my mother queries what this perspective entails and for a moment the moustache pontificates. He goes on to take Angelou to the Artic—to Churchill to see the polar bears and Eskimo children tossed in blankets. But their peculiar junket of a marriage comes to an abrupt end when Dwayne disappears. He's believed to have taken one of his elephant guns (which may be why I can't picture his head) and gone off to find another perspective. He would've happily given me a genuine pig-sticker bayonet from an Enfield rifle if my mother had let him, but I had to settle for a gleaming brass .300 Holland and Holland cartridge, a miniature golden rocket (that was later stolen during a birthday party by either Bill Bippus or Snotty Clark).

I like to think that a Komodo dragon got Dwayne. Or a charging Cape buffalo. He'd have preferred it that way. His disappearance left a hole much bigger than his body. In a world of three-bean salad and *The Donna Reed Show*, his stories of white slavery and bird-eating spiders had great resonance for me. Angelou soldiered on with admirable dignity and more than a little success with men, including a handsome Dutch carpenter who lived in Oakland and had marks on his arms from a childhood spent in a Nazi concentration camp. Then a car accident near Martinez changed her life forever and almost killed Gaja and Aunt Mabo.

Gaja lived with us. Aunt Mabo lived in a little stucco and terracotta Spanish duplex on Dartmouth Street off San Pablo, the long, blue-collar, fast-food and car-lot clogged artery that runs from the old shipyards and oil refineries of Richmond to the Oakland City Hall. One night a delivery boy ("Don't cook tonight, call Chicken Delight") was stabbed outside my aunt's door by a man in a porkpie hat who in turn was struck and killed by a Checker cab (her neighbor, Mr. Hornady, said the attacker was "high on goofballs after knocking over a greasy spoon").

I see Aunt Mabo standing with her gentleman-bandit husband at the center of the whole clan on that side of the family. He's a head taller than everyone else, wearing a tweedy English country squire hunting jacket, with a self-satisfied ambassadorial moustache and an immensely charming but deeply suspicious twinkle in his eye. There's a pervasive sepia mist about the picture . . . linen, wicker . . . babies in sailor suits. Shadows in a garden one summer long ago.

After his death, Aunt Mabo lived alone in Hartford for another ten years before moving out west to join her sister and to eventually become a second grandmother to me, famous for her white plastic "popcorn" beads that I liked to pull apart, and cinnamon doughnuts that she sliced sidewise and toasted under the griller (the doughnuts were purchased from Ortman's Bakery on Solano, which had the double advantage of being next door to a pet shop with a boa constrictor in a tank in the window).

It was a disturbing thing to see Gaja and Aunt Mabo after the accident, two old women bruised as if they'd been viciously beaten. But Angelou's injury was more serious still. She lost her left arm at the elbow. There was just a stump. I can see the color of it now. Dead pink pale hospital flesh. Not baby colored but injury colored—like burned people—like survivors who aren't sure they're glad they've survived. You notice a person's gestures more when they no longer have a forearm and hand. Your eyes try to complete the picture. Her nervous system did the same. Phantom limb pain. Negative space.

There was nothing simple about Angelou's response to her loss—or maybe that's what got her through. I only know that well before I'd have adjusted to such an obstacle, she was back nursing and exercising. After my mother asked my grandmother to leave and our family started falling apart, Gaja moved to an apartment on Oxford Street, which had a small pool. I can see Angelou plowing relentlessly up and down in that churning green rectangle, the echoing room reeking of chlorine and humidity, her artificial arm waiting on a chair by the door.

Then another picture—of her graduation from the Arthur Murray Dance Studio classes. Soon she'll go to a dude ranch, where she'll meet Floyd, a former construction worker who fell fifty feet off a scaffold and lived to tell the tale (again and again and again). He received an injury pension and became a Pentecostal Christian. Together they'd marry and move through years and pictures . . . from a duck farm in Solvang to a cottage in Ukiah to a camper out in the Mojave Desert (connected with a community with a religious fixation on the Palomar Observatory) . . . finally to a cabin in Bellows Falls, Vermont (during which time they won the New Hampshire state lottery and invested in a fully fitted-out Gospel Teen touring bus and led a group of young Christian singers around America to raise money for Oral Roberts University in Tulsa, two years after Roberts claimed he could raise the dead). I think of the picture of Angelou proudly waving her prosthetic limb from the Prayer Tower.

Located in the center of the campus to symbolize that prayer is of uttermost importance, the 200-foot Prayer Tower serves as the visitor center. The outward thrust of the observation deck represents the crown of thorns worn by Jesus Christ on the cross, and the red color represents the blood that was shed at His death. Atop the Tower, the eternal flame represents the baptism of the Holy Spirit. On the ground level visitors can view the Journey into Faith or browse in the gift shop.

No, there was nothing simple about her life. Always giving money and time and love to those she thought needed it. Floyd moved on to the great Mobile Home Park in the Sky and she moved back to a mobile home park in Redding, donating her time and money to her church and Sunday school and the local senior's center before succumbing to bowel cancer.

I confess I was always deeply irritated or amused by her, but when I think back on her life, I can't help but be impressed by her simple courage, if simple it was. No matter what her limitations, she was utterly sure that she was a daughter of God. There was certainly some presence looking out for her, watching over her life. I go back to the picture of her and Dad and my grandparents on the bench beneath the maple—the unknown boy stopped in the shade, looking on. He's still standing motionless in the shadow of the tree but I see him differently in this light. Before, he's always seemed vaguely sinister, a foreshadowing of the problems to come. Now I begin to wonder if this mysterious observer wasn't/isn't more a beneficent, protective presence. And I notice that perfectly balancing the figure in waiting in the shadows on the viewer's left is an orchardist's ladder on the right-hand side—a ladder that looks archetypally white compared with the receding blackness of the maple.

As I stare at the family flanked by shadow and ladder now, it suddenly occurs to me that Angelou is old enough and pretty enough in a bashful sort of way to be the source of this boy's attention. Perhaps he's not a friend of my father's so much as a friend of hers. Maybe the lip-biting shyness in her smile is a sign of a secret after all. There were always men in her life . . . and adventures . . . and miracles of sorts. I'm tempted to say, what explanation could be simpler? But I know to beware of anything that seems simple. There's always something that lies just out of frame.

SUNDAY ROAST

It irks me how my aunt tries to hack at her roast beef with her prosthetic arm. I hate the way it clunks on the table and makes the yellow Jell-O salmon quiver.

I wish my father would slice up the meat for her, but my sister and I have been told it's important that she does it for herself, even if she does clump and make the table shake.

At least the gelatin fish won't need a knife. It looks like it could tremble apart if I stared at it hard enough.

But the sickly yellow of the wobbling sugar crystal, my aunt's peach polyester dress, the brown of the gravy and the candy-corn orange of the boiled dead carrots can't be the colors of any Sunday dinner that would make you hungry.

My aunt uses her moving hand to wipe some gravy from her pale pink plastic one.

"Open your eyes," my mother says to me. "We've already said grace."

Then she takes a dull silver wedding spoon and scoops off the head of the glistening lemon-flavored salmon.

Or maybe it's a carp. A big yellow goldfish that can't hold still long enough even to disappear.

BLUE TO LIFE

I could tell you about my vague recollection of shaking hands with Martin Luther King . . . the sweltering summer of the 1967 riots in Detroit . . . my father preaching in a dead-cat-and-abandoned-needle parking lot . . . our windshield shattered with a brick . . . my mother screaming, "Why did you bring us here?"

It actually wasn't that much different than what was happening in Berkeley, tear gas drifting down the street . . . the National Guard deployed in force on the campus of the university . . . and across the bay at San Francisco State. Sit-ins, love-ins . . . strange ceremonies and costumes that seemed as if a book of fairy tales had exploded . . . enchantment turned to madness . . . the wonder of PF Flyers (the shoes that make you jump higher and run faster) and Jonny Quest decoder rings gone to the sudden seed of windblown fear and psychedelic desperation . . . the normalcy of Swanson TV dinners, with turkey and gravy and cranberry cobbler, becomes head wounds, gunshots, water cannons, flags and fire.

But the mind, like my family, clings to innocence, even in the face of whirlwinds. Especially in the face of whirlwinds. Cyclones of mirrors.

I'll tell you about my earliest remembered dream instead. I'm alone in bed and seemingly fast asleep when I feel myself called to. Something or someone is in the room. It's been there for a while. Watching me. Calling me with its silence. Gradually it's made me aware of itself—as if turning up the volume on its presence until I can no longer resist. Facing the wall, I have to slowly wake, swimming to the surface from a great depth.

I'm filled with an unspeakable wonder and dread. When at last I turn, for it seems to take the whole of my remembered life or no time at all—I find myself looking into the eyes of a Face staring at me out of a fine mist filling the room—the same unearthly blue as the picture of Jesus my grandfather painted, which hangs in the hall . . . a shade he called isle blue and used in many of his paintings and illustrations . . . between haint blue and cobalt, but somehow paler yet more vivid, as if lacings of metal trace have made it both more substantial and more opaque.

The Face isn't clearly a man's or a woman's—which disturbs and intrigues me. The body is naked, I think, and moist, but somehow receding, like breath on a mirror. It seems to lie *behind* the Face in another dimension rather than below, supporting the head. The presence fills the entire room now—I'm both inside it and outside. It doesn't speak to me aloud but I know that I must look. There's something blank and remote about the eyes, but nothing necessarily malevolent. Staring at it is strangely soothing. I want to look deeply, the way you sometimes want to drink too deeply from a water fountain on a hot day. Solely through the power of its unwavering gaze, the Face seems to be handling me, as you would a kitten or a puppy—carefully but not delicately. I can no more scream out than I can glance away. I remember nothing else other than the faint blue glow of the mist until I wake the next morning, the sun pouring through the curtain, everything exactly as it was—the maroon Naugahyde toy chest with the sailboat pattern unmoved. Everything unmoved but me—still transfixed by the Face . . . that nameless, blue, secret, swimming Face.

The same blue as the rubber safety handle of the Blue Diamond hammer Mr. Wyman later buys for me—the man who built our tree house at the cabin in Tahoe. He gives me a canvas bag with a diamond and a pine needle printed on it, a nail apron to tie around my waist so I can look like a carpenter too. He's one of Dad's "counselees" . . . he has problems.

In the one black-and-white photograph I have of him, he stands with his hands in the back pockets of his work pants, house painter's cap pushed back on his head, horn-rimmed glasses. His T-shirt is so white it looks like the negative space where his chest used to be, floating up through ponderosa pines, the platform that will become the floor of the tree house like a deer hunter's stand, almost invisible in the branches, where my sister with rabbit teeth and me with a bowl haircut sit Indian style at his feet. His voice has a warble or tremor to it, and even seemingly suspended in the space of pine bough and scattered sunlight (it strikes me as mysterious now how the photo was even taken), he looks like the perennial handyman—someone out of a poem by Robert Frost.

Ageless, thick of eyebrows and lean and wiry of frame, he shows me how to swing my blue-handled hammer, driving nails into boards, trees, the off-cuts of his efforts, which have a sweet, pungent scent to the shavings. All the valley smells of it, as building goes on all summer. Sprawling cedar homes, ski lodges or A-frame cabins like ours . . . my father's dream . . . he calls it Alpenglow . . . just off the Fallen Leaf Lake Road (which doesn't get plowed in winter, so the land was cheaper and we had to ski in) . . . seven acres of ponderosa pine, sugar pine and Jeffrey pine (the bark of which smells like vanilla), aspens and skunk cabbage. This is the place and the moment we will all love above all else and lose . . . my sister's and my ascension in the trees the perfect perspective and symbol of all that can't be sustained.

Poor Mr. Wyman, who gave me the hammer with a handle as blue as Pyramid Lake and a stiff white sailcloth bag for nails, ran the elevator in the Campanile on the campus at Cal Berkeley, the grand phallus of bell tower looming over the university, where if you looked quickly on the way up or down you could catch glimpses of the marvels stored on the other floors . . . pieces of dinosaurs . . . old theater costumes . . . swords and Gold Rush tools.

When he wasn't pounding nails and floating up through pines in someone else's summer photos, maybe the work in the bell tower wasn't so good for him . . . because he ended up committing suicide . . . jumping off the roof of one of the other buildings that he had the key to . . . he didn't want to risk landing on someone from the Campanile. After that, they put up heavy glass reinforcement to make it almost impossible.

The tree house that he built for us still stands, and with my blue hammer, I took to pounding hornets, scooping yellow jackets from the surface of the bathtub the horses would drink from and crushing them (until I was swarmed and stung close to twenty times and almost died).

Like the cabin . . . those summers . . . our lives together . . . and Mr. Wyman himself . . . the blue hammer seems to dissolve in my hand . . . leaving only blue . . . the same blue the dog turned that morning on the road to Minden, Nevada, my father at the wheel of our blue Impala . . . the backseat and trailer filled with a summer's worth of trash . . . from Cragmont cream soda cans to punctured archery targets.

We're driving to the dump in the cool of the early morning and Dad is thinking about fishing the Carson River on the way back . . . buying a salt lick for the horses, a heavy tongue-pink cube with the image of a mountain embossed on it. Somewhere along the way, there's a blue Ford pickup with a golden Labrador retriever in the bed, and cans of Sherwin-Williams paint, which I know from the huge neon globe down by the Aquatic Park in Emeryville, just off the Nimitz Freeway back home . . . all night a can of neon paint spills over the giant egg of the world and the lighted sign says WE COVER THE EARTH.

Suddenly, the truck swerves and rolls. Terrible twist and crunch of metal, branches scraping, grit of gravel . . . and my father spins the wheel. We crank back free into the morning shadow-blue of road, the trailer almost jackknifed but the hitch still intact. The truck plunges over the shoulder toward the river and I'm thinking that the dog is dead . . . but it finally bounds up through chokecherry barking blue . . . its coat stained a spirit unnatural dog color, and my father is flagging down a westbound truck to call for an ambulance, the wet blue of the dog all over my hands . . . all over my hands . . .

The same blue as the blue elephant keys they give to us kids at the zoo—big plastic skeleton keys with elephant handles that you insert in the speaker boxes beside each of the cages, which tell you a story about the animal inside.

The same blue as the background of the Blue Devil Fireworks stand in Yuba City, where the man with the retarded son sells Roman candles, skyrockets and sparklers . . . or the eyes of the chief in the Indian head of the Washoe Motel sign out on Highway 50.

It's the same blue as the sky of Reno the night we drive my aunt and uncle to catch the train at the end of summer and we stop for dinner at a place called the Persian Room.

Like everywhere in Nevada, the place had slot machines and I was walking past one, going to the bathroom, proud to be going by myself—looking down at the patterns in the carpet—and without thinking about it, I pulled down a handle. I guess someone had left money in that machine, which mustn't happen very often. But I pulled the silver arm down and three bright blue watermelons, those bizarre blue fruit you only find in gambling machines, cranked into the window with a satisfying whir and clunk. Jackpot. Twenty dollars. *Jackpot!*

A bell rang, and all of a sudden, change started cascading out—clanking wonderfully harsh and loud in the fat lip of the metal coin tray below. I froze, not knowing what to do. All the waitresses were dressed as belly dancers and one of them shimmered up to me. She was black and dressed in a gauzy, cloudy-blue veil covered with tiny bangles that caught the light. Her breasts were the biggest I'd ever seen. She leaned down to talk to me. She seemed so utterly real and yet I expected her to disappear in a wisp of smoke like a genie.

"You've got the luck," she whispered and put her hand on me.

She touched me and we got a shock—a spark of electricity there in that blue hallway. She took me back to our table and she touched me again without my parents seeing. It embarrassed me because it reminded me of the woman who touched the hem of Jesus's garment. And yet it thrilled me down deep in my little-boy loins. I can feel the cool blue fever of her even now.

The black lady is long gone. And the little white boy too. Only the blue remains.

DUST MELODY

I spent ages fascinated beyond measure by dust motes in the sunlight, lying on the floor next to Helen, my mother's accompanist. O mio babbino caro. The music of dust—female feet in white and oxblood pumps working the pedals . . . my mother barefoot when she sang . . . the rhythmic streaming of endless miniature worlds.

Helen's husband was a chemist for Shell and only drank milk, never alcohol. He played golf with my father, but didn't seem much interested in the game. He liked to disappear off into the rough to collect lost balls. He'd recovered over five thousand golf balls over the years. He kept them in a closet in the garage, all freshly washed and piled in buckets, labeled with the name of the golf course where he'd found them.

They had a son who had a problem. They bought him a Lionel model train set to keep him occupied. He liked his trains. His green felt town. His certain little world.

Until something would go wrong around the water tower or the cattle crossing and then there'd be screaming. My mother would have moved away from opera to songs from musicals, like "Stranger in Paradise," and suddenly a window would shatter upstairs. The golden dust of her singing would shudder and change shape, tiny pine trees and plastic cows flittering by the bay window, landing on the lawn. Then boxcars, flatcars, tanker cars smashing apart on the grass so that it looked like it had been raining model trains.

They always bought him new cars. They had the window fixed and fixed.

And every time there was an interruption, my mother would pause for a moment, as if she were waiting for the golden rivers of worlds to settle back into their steady dreaming—my little hands reaching through the bars and beams, amazed the whirling planets of dust could explode so softly and still heal back into their orbits, their flowing fall. Not like glass. Not like shark-nose locomotives or red cabooses. Like music I could hold.

SOLDIER IN THE EGG

All I could make of my cousin's ravings was something about inspecting the Zone and collecting the dead snakes. Then I dreamed myself . . . of animals thrashing in a net made of something they couldn't see. They were dying on a playground, I think—because of my confusion about the jungle—the only one I'd ever seen then was a jungle gym. My mother found me shivering in damp sheets.

I never told her the secret of my sympathetic delirium. I never even told my cousin Steve, the malarial Marine just home from Vietnam. But that afternoon, the nurses at Oak Knoll Naval Hospital had let me sponge him in his drowning.

He lay on his wet white bed in the room with drawn blinds, ranting about *rock apes butchered by automatic fire*—by which I came to understand he meant his platoon taking M-16s to the local baboons.

Only there are no baboons in Vietnam; they live in Africa. I'd find out years later that rock apes were some kind of legend that circulated among the soldiers. Maybe they were just monkeys that got blown away in fits of fear. Even Special Forces heroes lose their heads. But I believed him.

Finally, he fell asleep, gathering strength for another bout with the chills—the crossfire of a gunshot wound and the mosquito-borne blood disease. When his breathing slowed and his muscles relaxed, I dripped a drop of sweat from his navel into mine, and smeared it for the dark war magic I imagined.

I was young enough to believe that sharing the fever would help cure his purple heart.

CALL TO WORSHIP

Come dusk and the white gnats, my father would muster the fishing gear and fade into a pale aurora of wild carrot and gin. To stand, no, to sway—his heart at home in the perfect, dynamic monotony of the river.

He was a hard man to admire, but coming upon him in the midst and the mist of fishing, it was impossible not to be awed. I'd watch him silently, never even whistling—not so much standing on ceremony, as momentarily rooted in it.

He was a fisherman of fossils and artifacts too. Trilobites, tree rings and Oligocene insects inside eggs of amber. When the trout weren't biting, we looked for arrowheads. Because the secret of the past, he was fond of saying, is a fern frond pressed in a book of stone, at the bottom of what was once a lake of dreams.

Old man, young boy . . . there was always a lake of dreams.

DON'T GET A GUN, GET A BIG DOG

"*Lor-raine?* Is that you?" my mother asks.

She knows that the shadow almost out of sight on the second flight of our staircase isn't my grandmother.

She knows, but she feels obliged to ask out of some misguided, middle-class faith in the normality of afternoon sunlight.

I'm playing on the floor with a plastic fire truck and my sister's black patent-leather shoes. Not for long. My mother bundles us up without a word—me still clutching at the hot red plastic—my sister aware of an "emergency," mature in spite of herself.

We head straight to the Gages, the big Catholic family next door. Soon, Sandy Gage is telephoning the police and we're hiding at the window, waiting.

I watched him scale our backyard fence, a vindication of all the invisible evils I had warned my parents about, only to be dismissed as a child with a wild imagination. But there he was. At last, a monster of sorts—escaping, yes, but finally after others had seen him too.

And what a monster for a sunny afternoon.

He'd been there the whole time. He'd heard our pet names for ourselves. He knew that we were having Veal Birds in Bacon for dinner. He even knew of my impending birthday. And we knew nothing of him, except that he could stand very still, and that when we believed we were alone together—happy and sure of the familiarity of our lives, he was waiting on our back stairs.

I think my mother cried the first time I searched for a trace of his shadow. I admit I was standing at the window with the others when we watched him hop our fence. But having seen his shadow on the wall where my height was measured with pencil marks each birthday—how could I be sure he was gone? How could I be sure he was gone for good?

THE GHOSTS AND VAN CHEESE

I don't think you could've had a better big sister. I can't imagine one.

Back in the National Velvet In Search of Castaways Patty Duke past, she could draw well and was intensely inventive on a wide range of fronts. She created an entire scouting movement that included us and all the animals in the family and so was appropriately called Animals Combined (Cat Mandy, who gave birth to kittens Midnight and Wigwam, which for a while we got to keep . . . our German shepherd and dachshund . . . and John the Baptist, a box turtle, who was unfortunately flushed down the toilet during a mismanaged tank clean, for which I hang my head in shame). Each member had a special sash that she sewed, and there were literally hundreds of colorful merit badges to earn that she both invented and made by hand. And what unique ideas for merit badges. There was one that mixed rock-climbing with archery, and another that united puppet theater with safety. That was very much like my sister then—creating whole new categories of achievement. How many scouting programs do you know that reward you for remembering your dreams?

I got my first badge for saying "Fuzzy Wuzzy Was a Bear, Fuzzy Wuzzy Had No Hair, Fuzzy Wuzzy Wasn't Fuzzy, Was He?" to bald Mr. Webb before I started laughing and ran away.

My sister was always fair. Our German shepherd received a merit badge for fishing when she leapt out of the boat with Dad in Angora Lake just as he was reeling in what he said was a monster steelhead but what was really a small rainbow (the dog helped Dad earn his boat rescue badge, too).

In my sister's hands, our murky staircase (perfect for letting a Slinky down) turned into the Zambezi River, complete with waterfalls, pythons, pygmies and poison arrows. (Later, when the TV show *The Time Tunnel* came on, I once wrapped myself in a sheet and hurled myself down those stairs, hoping that I might find myself back at Gettysburg or in the Coliseum in Rome.)

My sister supervised my collections of rocks and minerals, seashells and belly button lint. She sewed two odd teardrop-shaped pillow creatures that were sort of like Laurel and Hardy. She was a wizard with Pig Latin, and once, when she found some vitamin E pills, she told me there were little skin divers inside so I spent hours staring at them with a magnifying glass. Like a blend of Hayley Mills (who was my first love) and Tintin, she was truly a savant and a leader.

She had a huge crush on James Drury, the star of *The Virginian*, and made the whole family go see him at a big horse show in the Cow Palace. She taught me the legend of Falling Rock in the backseat of our Rambler on our summertime travels. She showed me the key on the $1 bill. She taught me tiddlywinks, Red Light Green Light, Yahtzee—and songs like "Little Rabbit Foo Foo" and of course . . . *On top of Spaghetti, all covered with cheese, I lost my poor meatball, when somebody sneezed.*

She included me in all her playtime adventures with her friend Poppy (although one of the prices for this privilege was that they dressed me up like a girl once, complete with makeup and earrings, and made me climb up on the roof to retrieve their Wiffle ball).

And she was an early mix master on the vinyl record scene, demonstrating how on *Bozo the Clown Under the Sea* (an old 78 record) the voice of the Swordfish sounded like God when played at 33 rpm—or what we imagined God sounded like anyway. (*Seventy-eight records*, I hear you say . . . yes, well, in those days there were more things from other eras just lying around, although they were disappearing as we touched them, which is perhaps why we attached special value to them.)

My sister was more or less the secretary of entertainment for the family and was famous for her four-year-old rendition of Tennessee Ernie Ford's "Sixteen Tons" in pink pajamas (which I'm very sorry I missed, although I did get to hear her do the theme song to *77 Sunset Strip*). By the time I came along, we were of course inundated with Elvis and the Beatles, as was every other household in America, but we were honestly more partial to Herman's Hermits and Chubby Checker (both of us were pretty good twisters—or rather I became a good twister under her direction). Our mutual favorite, though, was Dusty Springfield.

My sister had a little white suitcase record player and would play "I Only Want to Be with You" and dance to it while I climbed onto my squeaky rocking horse in my sleepers and enjoyed a kind of controlled epileptic swoon. It was a very bizarre sensation that overcame me then. A rise of adrenalin and probably a release of endorphins. Like the rush of possibility kids get on big ion days when it's windy and warm—that sweet, sharp hint of ozone. I was intensely susceptible to this from my earliest memories, and music could simulate it. Early morning cirrus cloud hopefulness—or thunderstorm joy. My first sense of being high. And I think the first hint of the sexual buzz. We'd rock out and I'd ride like the little boy in "The Rocking Horse Winner," forever gaining on some longed-for destination I had no idea about, only certain it was a kind of victory and deep knowing.

My sister had a special fascination for John Glenn, and, I believe, had she set her mind to it, she'd have made a fine space explorer (not to mention sinister mastermind or international spy). There was at that stage in our lives virtually nothing she couldn't have done if the fit had taken her. She had more ideas than most R&D departments of the day.

Every Christmas, she'd read aloud the story called "Why the Chimes Rang." And she read a lot to me generally—stories like "Thumbelina" and "William Tell" and other tales from our Childcraft books (her favorite being "Bunny the Brave," about a rabbit who outsmarts a vicious tiger, tricking him with his reflection in a pool of water). She wasn't beyond occasionally taunting me, however, and one of the vehicles she deployed with deftness was a Time-Life coffee-table book on the wonders of the universe, which began with the immensely influential dinosaur illustrations of Charles R. Knight. (It's hard to think of an artist who's had more impact on both science and popular culture.) I naturally loved them. There's something about giant reptiles and huge-eyed amphibians with dagger teeth. Those paintings opened up vast new vistas and formed an interesting contrast to the other two obsessive fascinations of the period: cowboys and space. Cowboys wrangling dinosaurs on distant planets (or in Live Oak Park) became a staple fantasy.

I see now that what unites them is some imagined sense of frontier. What I only implicitly appreciated was the aspect of nostalgia. A brontosaurus, six guns and a jet car . . . cavemen, box canyons, satellites . . . it was all the same dream really. Escape from the post-Eisenhower doldrums and the emerging tide of strangeness. A grasping at the future while clinging to the past . . . while reality slipped further away. My belief now is that all these luxuriant plastic growths and contagions were the aftershocks of Hiroshima and Nagasaki that shook our school and home windows like the sonic booms of those days (when's the last time you heard a sonic boom?). The Cold War and the Dick Clark disease of television go claw in glove. A rain of lunchboxes fell out of those mushroom clouds. Dolls and dinosaurs . . . ray guns—fake Winchester rifles. I had a silver pistol that offered me gamma and beta ray options—and a pump-action toy shotgun "good for varmints" that was so loud I had to ask permission to fire it. "Becout, Mommy." Boom. But I especially liked the megafauna in the Time-Life book—giant ground sloths in particular. I wanted very much to have a giant ground sloth—and I had the name all picked out. Beauregard.

Where things got a little edgier was where the photographs started. There was one—it took up a full page and was a source of amazement and total terror—and my sister knew it. The giant grouper, which changes sex from female to male—and that poignant line "has been known to eat small boys whole." She could always get me with the giant grouper, and my own fixation on trying to confront the fear only made it more powerful. Time and again I'd sneak peeks at that fat, suckered face, hoping to be able to stare down that brute—but I couldn't. The page was too big and I felt swallowed whole every time.

My sister got me hooked on the *World Book Encyclopedia* and presided over our collection of story records, which she taught me to play on my own. So I came to be friends with Ebenezer Scrooge, Huckleberry Finn, Lancelot and Guinevere, the Prince and the Pauper, and the Swiss Family Robinson. The story record we both enjoyed the most, however, was a Walt Disney creation that brought together the two great Washington Irving tales *Rip Van Winkle* and *The Legend of Sleepy Hollow*, which you'd have to say have never gone out of fashion.

The character voices were superb and the music was a major improvement on what appeared in the cartoon movies. What really got us, though, was "The Headless Horseman Song," in which Brom Bones famously terrorizes Ichabod Crane, knowing he can scare the bejesus out of him to keep him from winning the attention of Katrina Van Tassel. *Along about midnight, the ghosts and Van Cheese get together for their nightly jamborees . . .*

I'd have to say this was a defining story in our lives. *For once you cross the bridge, the ghost is through, his power ends.* You can never be sure if Ichabod is pursued by the mutilated rider who haunts the old Dutch countryside of the Hudson River Valley, and everyone who's been there knows just what an odd locale it is (and anyone who knows Dutch people knows how odd they are)—or if the whole awful ordeal is a well-played but pretty mean prank by Brom Bones. The desire to believe in the Headless Horseman—the supernatural evil—works hard against the mundane explanation. (A tension I'd have quite a bit to do with, as it turns out.)

When the eerie laughter and the music began, I'd get on my rocking horse and start frantically riding for the bridge. It was a trance state that took over my whole body, producing an intense erection and electrifying the hairs on the back of my neck—a delirious high like unto a drug, if I'd known then what drugs were like.

With a hip-hip and a clippity-clop
He's out looking for a head to swap
So don't try to figure out a plan
You can't reason with a headless man.

But as scary as Brom Bones and the Headless Horseman were, my sister and I both lived in dire, glorious fear of Van Cheese—picturing him as the awakened corpse of some ghastly, slobbering, burlap-headed Dutch renegade soldier from the Hessian or War of 1812 times . . . a vast, rotting presence, lord of spirits and convener of dark ceremonies. It would be many, many years and strange, dark ceremonies of our own before we'd realize that the words we both heard and came to sing along to in our exuberant terror—the name and the dreadful ghoulish presence it inspired—was all a misunderstanding.

Along about midnight it wasn't the ghosts and Van Cheese who came out for their fiendish fun—it was the ghosts and *banshees.* A much different proposition. I think both of us are glad we didn't know that then. We would've missed a delicious fright that we could actually savor.

The curious thing is that we both knew what banshees were—even me. We were rather well versed in magical beings in our house. But it says something about the nature of perceptions, families and how mythologies grow, that for years the specter of Van Cheese loomed in our living room. I've often wondered since if what would happen later was foreshadowed in this imagined predator. Or does a shared mistake reveal a family tendency to personify darkness—and so to call it forth? Maybe what we fantasized Van Cheese to represent is always there, in every living room, waiting to take shape and give new shadow to midnight, whenever summoned by either vulnerability or desire. And perhaps those two states of being are but different names for the same thing if we delved deeper. I think back to my rocking . . . the as-yet undefined blur between ozone excitement, fear, erotic stimulation, hunger, longing, innocence, greed—both pursuit and escape. In any case, we lived for what seemed like then eternity and now but a moment, in a conspiracy of improvisation and invention, when we weren't lost in *The Wonderful World of Disney*, *Honey West* and *Hawaiian Eye.*

CUCKOO

Some things just can't be talked about. So they end up taking on a peculiar life of their own. Alicia Sandringham, for example.

She was an energetic, eccentric woman who supported our church and was one of the family's "benefactors." (We needed several of these because of the way my parents managed their money.) She'd inherited a considerable fortune from her father, who was a big hardware merchant back in Illinois, and she was intent on doing good with some of those substantial proceeds.

As a dedicated Christian woman, this would lead her to Africa, where she founded a literacy center in what was then Rhodesia. She helped out in the villages. She washed babies. She built a medical clinic . . . and twice a year, she came back to the house she maintained in the Berkeley Hills, which she let my father and mother use for church functions, provided a stout, nervous man named Mr. Sewickley was informed.

Alicia Sandringham was over six feet tall, was in her late fifties, and had never been married. She had thick, short hair that reminded me of an eraser on the end of a pencil. She was a powerful but not necessarily tuneful singer, yet she was a bastion of my mother's choir and I think may have contributed to my mother's tuition when Mom went back to the university for a graduate degree.

All these things I came to understand over time, but what I could see for myself were the pictures that remained in the house . . . many photographs over many years, of her and an African woman whose name I couldn't pronounce. They'd met in Berkeley, where the woman was studying. The idea of going to Africa came out of the relationship with this woman, what my mother called Alicia's "lifelong friend." Even in Berkeley it was necessary then to disguise certain things—or to seek greater freedoms far away. I see it pretty clearly now. There's no mistaking particular postures and expressions between two people—especially not when there are many photographs to examine. Two strong women, both never married, the difference in race and culture only seeming to make their connection more complementary. One tall, thin and white . . . the other round, buxom and black. Subdued, mute masculine clothes . . . bright-colored female robes.

But of course, they were both fervent Christians, doing God's work in a developing country, so nothing was ever said. And I don't think that this had anything to do with us kids being too young to understand—because I, at least, did understand, in some unspoken, child-savant way. I could read the photographs. Although my family, like many, was obsessed with photographing our lives, few of those pictures were ever really looked at, to see what story they told. Once captured, the moments actually faded. Anything not intentional, not posed, became invisible. Life lived this way has a curious tendency to become even more dreamlike than it is. An alternative world takes shape around all the things unacknowledged.

Looking back now, I think how much better it would've been if my family could've openly accepted the nature of Alicia's life, Christianity and all, and not ignored it through a superficial politeness or supposed respect for privacy. Children aren't that easy to fool. I may not have understood the details, but I had a keen sense of the underlying reality. I believe this is innate in most children generally. The question then becomes to what extent the instinct is nurtured or suppressed. Oddly, it may be nurtured *because it's suppressed.* It becomes a method of psychic self-defense. I'm fairly sure this is what happened in my case.

I came to see Alicia's home as a haunted house. If she was robust and always beaming, with tales of life in Africa upon her annual returns, there was about the empty place when she was gone a deeper emptiness than met my parents' eyes. White linen laid over furniture, a stale fragrance of dust and silence, punctuated only by the click-click-clicking of the ornate cuckoo clock in the living room, which Mr. Sewickley, Alicia's neighbor and caretaker, kept continuously ticking, even when she was away.

He was a man you could never imagine having been young. Plump, always overdressed—with soft, oily hands that he powdered with talc. "Fastidious" my mother called him. He lived alone in a big house two doors away, and as far as I knew, his chief occupation in life was making sure the cuckoo clock kept working, tinging out the hours in a house of ghostly sheets and photographs of black children far away.

The clock mesmerized me. It was unusually large—heavily carved and laden with all manner of frippery and trim. The numerals were impossibly intricate to read. Even the hands seemed overstated—and I was at the age when telling time was still an achievement, and I called the hands "arrows," which is more accurate.

Whenever we were over and Alicia was gone (which is a strange thing in itself), I took to climbing on top of a hassock and peering into the secret world inside the clock. What was going on inside between the hours? I imagined a complex inner life—a life every bit as mysterious as my own family's—and with reason.

Because on the hour, one of two figures would emerge through the little snap-shutting double doors with the gold filigree. On the even hours, a tiny woodsman would slide out on his chain-driven track and swing his axe to seemingly split a log, which would ring as if he'd struck a metal wedge. The number of blows denoted the number of the hours, and I was amazed for a long time that he knew exactly how many times to swing his axe.

I was even more mystified at first by his wife, who came out on the odd hours and rang a little circle of metal with a rod, as if calling the woodsman home to eat. This was the explanation my mother offered, but it didn't ring true to me. Why should she have to clink harder at 11 am than at 1 pm, which was more like lunchtime? More importantly, why did she need to call him at all, when I knew he was inside the house of the clock?

"Maybe he's lazy, and she's calling him out to chop more wood," my mother said.

Once I remember asking her, "Do we live inside a kind of clock too?"

I don't recall being satisfied with the answer I received.

It's funny how people resist precision and then worry about regularity and stability. (For a long time I associated the term *regularity*, which I often heard mentioned on TV, with the behavior of the woodsman and his wife in the cuckoo clock.) That was another thing. Why was it called a cuckoo clock? There was no little bird that popped out to screech or tweet. I felt the woodsman and his wife were living under false pretenses. The truth of their lives went unregarded despite their best efforts on the hour to demonstrate their existence. What more could they do? They were as faithful in the performance of their duties as anyone or anything could be, and often I would think of them, shuttling forth from their cozy house when no one was around to see or hear them—because Mr. Sewickley had shuttled forth from his house from time to time to insure they were still clicking and clinking.

I felt rather sorry for them, always working, always trying to prove they weren't cuckoos. I hoped their life inside the clock was more interesting, and I imagined all sorts of things that they'd get up to. What would a man and woman do all day inside a house that was a clock? I wondered why they didn't have any children, not knowing at the time anything about how children came to be—other than the fact that so many men and women seemed to have them. The woodsmen and his wife just appeared, like clockwork.

Becoming ever more puzzled by these questions, one afternoon prior to a Bible study class my mother had organized, once Mr. Sewickley had removed the white sheets from the furniture and dabbed himself with his handkerchief (which was like a little bed-sheet he carried in his pocket), I took off my shoes and climbed atop the hassock that I pushed into position, to make a closer inspection of the world of the timepiece's interior.

Of course it was always hard to see much through the itsy bitsy windows, and despite my fantasies, the evidence suggested the two figures didn't move much if at all inside—although I naturally found this very hard to believe. I felt somewhat guilty peeking, because I realized I very much wanted to know what was going on inside the houses around ours, but I knew without having to ask that peering in through the windows wouldn't be welcomed, regardless of the excellent reasons for wanting to do so. If it didn't seem right to peep into a house, it couldn't be right to peep into a house that looked like a clock. But I did anyway.

On this occasion, however, I somehow got too involved in my investigation and was caught by surprise when the hour struck. Out swept the woodsman's wife and startled me, so that in trying to avoid falling from the hassock, I grabbed the clock and the wife broke off into my hands.

Needless to say, I was worried. I knew instantly that Mr. Sewickley would be shaken from his track by the news. Some kind of punishment was inevitable. Perhaps I'd never be allowed to return. I'd almost assuredly be told to stay away from the clock from then on.

But in the moment, what was more on my mind was the woodsman's wife. When I looked down at the little carved wooden figure I held in my hand, I realized she wasn't a woman. She was simply the woodsman wearing a dress. It was the same figure, only in a different costume. I'd had some vague suspicions along these lines before, but I'd never been able to verify them. Up close and static now, it was obvious.

This reminded me that my sister had insisted once over Salisbury steak that Mr. Blaycock wore a dress (he lived three houses away from us with his cousin Ernest). She knew because she'd seen him in the window when she was selling mints for the Lions Club. Nothing more was said about this by our parents or grandmother, but my sister remained convinced.

Partly to try to take the focus off my damage to the clock, but more because I was genuinely flummoxed, I pointed out the likeness to my mother. She was upset with me and was bustling around getting teacakes and apple cider ready for the Bible study. She was in no mood to scrutinize the figure. Did this mean the woodsman really lived alone and sometimes came out wearing a dress?

"Don't be silly," my mother said. "You've caused trouble enough. It's the woodsman's wife. She's wearing a dress. The woodsman's still inside."

"But it looks *just* like the woodsman," I said. "It's the woodsman wearing a dress."

"It's just not a very good carving," she replied.

Five minutes later, she lied to Mr. Sewickley when he stuck his head back in. "Something happened to the clock," she said. "Hopefully, it's not permanent."

"This broke off," I said, a bit more truthfully, handing him the figurine.

He looked so mortified I thought he might've been broken too. I slipped away quickly into another part of the house, to look at the photographs of Alicia in Africa, smiling in front of a thatched hut and a portable concrete mixer beside her best friend.

THE EAR

Every perfect family needs a Shetland pony, right? Girls and horses. I missed my sister's doll era (I don't think she had much of one), but she was deeply committed to miniature horses. I'd say there were over a hundred by the time I could tie my shoelaces by myself. She kept them dusted with a moist washcloth every day. From there it seemed a natural evolution to getting her a real horse of some sort to ride. (I sorely wished this same principle had applied to my interest in robots.)

Our mother, who felt that horseback riding was the ideal way to emphasize what she considered her aristocratic bearing and patrician heritage, aided her in this scheme. (In truth, her father had just been a country doctor with a thick head of white hair and a modest talent on the viola, who'd inherited a big, drafty house full of chimney swifts and field mice—but in her mind it was a mansion on the hill, and she couldn't believe she'd given up a roomful of suitors bringing her corsages and had chosen my minister father, who tied fishing flies at the dinner table and did ridiculous imitations of Hitler with a black comb held above his upper lip, even if he hadn't been into the infamous cupboard where he kept his hooch.)

The family's fixation on horses (along with all their associated costs) would have some profound repercussions on our finances and solidarity when the divorce eventually happened (which was something like the earthquakes we experienced so often, only it didn't stop—it just kept shaking things apart). But the obsession started out modestly enough, with a Shetland pony ride at Tilden Park for my sister. I was quite happy to stick with the merry-go-round. (I particularly enjoyed riding the giant rooster, so perhaps I shouldn't make any comments about girls and horses.)

Of course worshipping miniature horses is one thing; actually getting on a slightly less miniature horse is another. My sister was petrified, which I found deeply amusing. Somehow, it seemed like such a long way to the ground to her—and yet she so wanted to be able to do it. Dad's solution was ever a lateral one (although many would've said "skewed").

One of his techniques for getting us over any fear of the water had been to blindfold us. As strange as that may sound, it had worked very well, and both my sister and I became good, fearless swimmers at a fairly young age. It was true that I was forced to wear a life preserver in open water like a lake, but even Dad occasionally employed some sensible precautions.

Seeing my sister's alarm at having her dream fulfilled, but worrying that she might wet her pants with anxiety on her first real ride, he took the pillowcase off one of the pillows we'd been sitting on the lawn with, and put it over her head. I think the people running the pony ride were rather surprised by this move—and I'm fairly certain several other parents were—to see this little girl wearing a white hood led around the ring on a pony. "Mommy, am I going to have wear one of those?" a girl behind me asked.

I see my sister parading around the circle of dust, looking like a kidnap victim or a Klan child undergoing some initiation rite.

My mother was scandalized (but that was easily done). Two circles around, and the hood came off. Dad's methods were unorthodox, but they worked.

After that success, for so it was counted, the next step was a true ride out in some fields and on a real trail. The "ranch" was out in Martinez, which is the seat of Contra Costa County (where I would later serve my only jury duty assignment, an interesting murder case that finally hinged on a photograph of a driveway where the outline of a car appeared, proving that it had been parked there during the rainstorm when the crime was committed). It's also the birthplace of Joltin' Joe DiMaggio and home to a massive Shell Oil refinery and tank farm that gives the live oak California ranchero air a distinct tinge of industrial grit.

But the pony farm my father located was there, and so off we went one Saturday. Everything seemed fine at the start. My sister was calm (and no doubt glad not to have to wear the pillowcase). The pony was a fat thing named Suzie and seemed smaller to me than most of the merry-go-round animals. I figured if I could ride a big crazy-looking chicken, my older sister could ride a half-pint horse. What could go wrong?

Well, that's the problem when things go wrong—it becomes very hard later to say where the drama started. Was it Dad's lack of attention to the security of the saddle when the woman with the big bazooms came out to water some of the other ponies? Was it her husband with the terrible stutter that put us all off? Was it the mix of gold grass and black oak pollen combined with the harsh waft of oil smoke and plastics being made? The fact that my mother had wrapped our crumbed chicken picnic in cellophane and not foil, which then peeled off the skin and meat, could've been a factor too. Maybe everything counts when an emergency transpires.

Maybe accidents don't just happen, but are delicately if secretly orchestrated.

What occurred in this case was something my sister would've been better off wearing her hood to have experienced. The pony got loose and shot forward at full gallop. That may sound funny, and the whole idea of ponies is indeed a bit foolish—but they're still powerful creatures, and this little tubby thing got up to speed in a way that stunned us all. My sister especially.

We watched her gallop off, just like in a movie. At first, I admit, I thought it was funny. There was an element of someone's hobby getting away from them—of life, even at pony size, being more than they bargained for. But there was an acute sense of our family running away from itself too. The shrill cry of my mother blaming my father, when it seemed to me that she was every bit as much at fault. The whole horse passion was really hers. And what good did it do to yell at him, anyway, when the problem was two hundred yards away and escaping? Without understanding it, I learned a vital lesson that afternoon. The first person to assign blame is the most likely to be at fault. Think about that when stuff happens. I've found it to be a very sound rule. "I thought your father had it all under control" are words that might ring across the ages and at least two of the major religions.

My father, for all his shortcomings, had a theological position that can be summarized as this: don't lose faith even when the blood starts to flow, and in this world, God's work must truly be our own. He leapt into our old Rambler and bounced across the fields around the back. Meanwhile, my sister had slipped from the saddle and appeared to be almost dragged along the ground, her head seeming to bounce even more than the car.

Dad returned about fifteen minutes later, leading the pony, with my sister back in the saddle, her face streaked red with tears and fear—and blood. He held something in his hand with an uncomfortable level of care.

Not two minutes later we were in the stuttering rancher's car and headed to the hospital. My sister was in a state of shock, holding the left side of her head. I wanted to hold the ear, which was wrapped in some of the cellophane left over from our picnic.

You think we might've learned from that episode, but not us. That was just the beginning.

I glanced at the ear in my mother's lap and noticed there was some chicken skin on the side of the transparent wrapping. It made me think of the mad rainbow-colored rooster I'd ride on at Tilden Park. We were all on a carousel, without even knowing it.

"It's only a piece of the ear," my father said to the rearview mirror. (He'd later do that even when the backseat was empty, old habit.) "It's going to be all right. They can do wonders now. Just some stitches."

"If I had a pony of my own, this would never have happened," my sister choked, in a brilliant seize-the-moment ploy. Dad would've handed her the car keys just then—anything to duck Mom's wrath. I, meanwhile, was wondering what an ear would taste like—figuring it would probably be a step up from my mother's chicken. We were all on the same carousel, lost in the same stampede.

"It's going to be all right," Dad repeated, and I knew that he'd say that at least five more times before we got home again.

SCHOOL FOR THE DEAD

There comes a morning when you're forced to realize reality is more than a triceratops you can hold in your hand. Not only must you go to the bathroom in a public place on your own—but you must go to school.

School was a mysterious thing to me, because my mother was a teacher, but way across town. In order to get there, we had to drive by the large School for the Deaf, which was the subject of a running joke in our family, in that I at first thought I'd heard School for the Dead, and I didn't think it was fair that dead children still had to go to school. This provoked great amusement among my family, which I didn't take kindly to at all.

My academic career got off to a rocky start. Thinking she was doing the right thing, my mother took me along to nursery school a year early, just to give me a taste of what lay ahead so as to ease the shock when I finally really did have to go. The teacher was an older woman who was more than a bit deaf herself (which is probably how she put up with the rambunctious kids—or maybe how she'd lost her hearing). She misunderstood, assuming I was merely a late entrant and shooed my mother away, leaving me stranded amid the squalling, jabbering riot—for the first naked time.

There are only a few trials in life to compare with that initial collision with the outside world. For me it was traumatic in the extreme. The apple juice and graham crackers helped considerably, as did gluing down a pelican made of peanut shells. I made it through, but I returned home to my grandmother Gaja with a sense of relief verging on the religious. I'd been given a reprieve. Another year of home and the private world I knew and cherished. Still, I'd seen the future and I realized it wasn't as overwhelming as I'd been afraid of.

In the intervening months, my perspective naturally changed further. What had previously been a nurturing and protective shell began to seem more and more restrictive. I came to feud more with my mother and even with Gaja. I bristled at the little-boy treatment. For the first time I started to give shape to the notion that I was being given two brutally opposed directives—one, to act very grown-up around grown-ups and, two, to never grow up, at least not in relation to other children my age. The first seeds of rebellion had been sowed. I became aware that my mother's baby talk, which I'd formerly either enjoyed and participated in or failed to notice, now very much annoyed me. I took a stand and formally stopped calling her Mommy. The adoption of "Mom" seemed like a big gesture at the time, and wasn't lost on her.

The other thing that changed me is that I technically was the one to find our neighbor Mr. Crawford dead in his garage (carbon monoxide poisoning). It happened during a game of hide-and-seek with my sister and the Gage kids next door, and it didn't really freak me out as much as it might seem. Not in the moment anyway. That's the thing about being a kid—or me as a kid—I could worry about our cleaning lady Grace, this sort of cunning, severe Japanese woman, turning into a giant slimy brown fish when you weren't looking—and then quickly changing back when you did—but dead Mr. Crawford only alerted me in an official way of something I should tell my sister about. I didn't quite understand what I'd glimpsed through the dirty window of the garage, except that it wasn't right . . . the car running . . . Mr. Crawford slumped over. His wife had died of lung cancer a month or so before. She'd been a very heavy smoker—I remember her once blowing smoke at me through their screen door (that was creepy). They were a childless couple in their late fifties . . . liked working on jigsaw puzzles together.

By the time I did have to go to nursery school, I was ready. There was a kid in my class who looked like Popeye, only he was black, and one who looked like Ernest Borgnine, and Tiger who wore only brown clothes—and a tall boy named Heinz who had accidentally been shot by his brother with a .22 and was always showing everyone the scar. Terry Sutcliffe, who wore a Beany and Cecil cap, poked me in the forehead with a pencil and left a blue mark that would stay there forever. We did the exercises with Jack LaLanne, who always wore weird stretch pants, and I hated Captain Kangaroo because I thought Mr. Greenjeans and Mr. Moose were dumb. One week I was ball monitor at recess and my hands smelled like rubber dodge balls. Adam and I wondered about the abandoned missile base in the hills and teased Eleanor Peacock, whose teeth were all rotten from sucking Fizzies. Becky Coyle, the jeweler's daughter, always dressed up like Little Bo Peep, while I always dressed up like a cowboy. Sometimes she came over to our house and liked to have me watch her when she sat on the toilet. Eric had a crush on Patricia, who was the first girl I ever liked too. The little buggy things that floated in your eyes when you looked up into the sky were space snakes—and if you turned your head upside down you could see Upside Down World, where you had to step over doorways and where chandeliers grew upwards like trees.

Generally speaking, nursery school and kindergarten were

pleasant experiences. I had a friend named Anthony, who I collected military badges with. We slid on wax paper down the cement slide at Codornices Park on Euclid Avenue, next to the Berkeley Rose Garden. As long as I could have my sofa pillow fights when I got home (and some time to look at my penis) I was OK.

But come first grade, things of course started getting more serious—in all ways. I stopped wearing my cowboy outfit, for starters. Then there was walking to school—which I did with my sister and two of the Gage kids. It was kind of exciting in the morning, and for the most part, my unexplained fears were under control. There was always a chance of crossing paths with FBI agents, the Abominable Snowman or the Scarlet Pimpernel (although I developed a curious terror of people wearing foam neck braces). There were the bells of fuchsia blossoms to burst and pyracantha berries to have fights with.

The Hilltop School was actually on a hilltop and had a good view east and west—with Indian paintbrush and California poppies all around. I liked gazing out toward the bay or over the hills—but to get to it from our house you had to make your way up through an older derelict school with boarded-up windows and peeling hallways. This didn't worry me in the mornings, but coming back home in the afternoon, I did worry. A lot. I could feel the presence of invisible children—I heard their voices. It was a haunted sense of the Other World that I had to walk right through. It both gave me the willies and moved me deeply, implanting a lifelong love of abandoned places, the continuous presence of the past that lies hidden just beyond immediate seeing.

At first I thought things were going to be all right. I took to the new, larger playground, the knock-knock and dead-baby jokes, the monkey bars, tetherball—and I liked listening to the girls' lemon-lime-be-on-time jump rope chants (although naturally nothing was said about that very openly). It was a very different world then. Kids still played jacks and we were allowed to carry pocketknives so we could play mumblety-peg. The school days had grown longer of course—there were bells ringing in the halls (there's something intrinsically jolting about school bells, and they always seemed especially loud to me)—and the energy of the other kids struck me as being a kind of storm. There was also the matter of simply spending more focused time with those my own age—not just hugger-muggering around on the swing sets or squealing through pin-the-tail-on-the-donkey party games—more coherent, attentive time—smelling them, examining the clothes they wore, what they carried for lunch. And hearing what they called going to the bathroom. Nothing quite launches the process of gaining some more objective perspective on your family than finding out how other families refer to the bodily functions. There's the sudden realization that your own family is different—and it's hard then not to wonder if the differences may extend more broadly still.

We didn't use the number 1 and number 2 code in our household. A fart was a "mouse in the house." Pissing was "going potty" or just "going to the bathroom," while shitting was "having a BM" (it would be many years before I understood the simple meaning of that term). The actual toilet was "the john."

I knew Becky Coyle talked of tinkling and pooing, but spending more time with a wider range of other kids made it clear just how many other names were used, and without quite seeing it clearly, I grasped in a subconscious way that our family had a degree of squeamishness about the whole issue. I also noticed that other kids made mention of the significant body parts much more often than my sister and I did. There was a vigor and a physicality in their speech that to my ears sounded crude and biting. They seemed to have more fun talking about such things—and that concerned me. For the first time,

I began to sense an ongoing effort on particularly my mother's part to discourage engagement with my peers. A subtle but constant family orientation existed, like a force field (and the term *force field* was all around us in space stories and on TV). There were things that were *dirty.* And that meant there were people who were dirty. There were things and people to be resisted.

I also was becoming aware of my peculiar attitudes toward food. Certain things revolted me beyond reason. Many kids are finicky eaters but I was unaccountably narrow in my choices. The smell of luncheon meats like bologna could make me vomit or squirm with repugnance. Mustard was unthinkable. Tuna fish would make me just plain run away. Basic fruits like apples and oranges that heaps of other kids loved—I couldn't cope with. A carrot or celery stick was out of the question. All I could handle for lunch was a peanut-butter-and-jelly sandwich, chocolate milk and a cookie. The rigidity of these views made it hard to share lunches with the other kids and further emphasized in my private mind that I was different—perhaps even doomed from the beginning. I just couldn't seem to be like other kids. I wanted to be—and yet I sensed my parents didn't want me to be. I didn't know what was the right way to behave—only that I wished for a world of crystal radio sets and battle with enormous carnivorous reptiles.

But of all the elements that added a new seriousness to reality, the most serious of all was my teacher, Mrs. Mauer. She was a towering woman of six feet, which seemed tremendously intimidating at my age, and she wore stiff, angular, masculine-looking suits that exaggerated her height still further. Unquestionably, she was the tallest and leanest woman I'd seen close up at that point, with skin as white as Elmer's glue. Her short red hair was cut like a man's and had two deep permanent waves that looked like molded Play-Doh (if she'd ever whipped off her hair like a cap, I for one wouldn't have been surprised). She had a vaguely German accent, which was itself somehow distressing. She also had an upper dental plate that lent to her speech an awkward lisping quality, which she then overcompensated for with a crispness of diction that made her sound always angry. And it wasn't just the fear of her temper that worked on us—there was Snip and Crack to worry about.

Teachers had a lot more freedom and a lot less scrutiny in those days. Things that went unnoticed then would never be tolerated today. Snip was her name for the pair of scissors she carried in the front pocket of her suit (all her suits—I think she only had three—had pockets seemingly designed specifically to carry this implement when it wasn't out and clicking). The blades were bright silver and the handle blood red, and she would use them like an insidious musical instrument to punctuate certain remarks. The practice may well have started as just a nervous habit, but she'd grown dependent on the scissors and was always brandishing them, slicing at the air in time with her words—or during quiet time, when we were practicing handwriting or working on a quiz—as an echo to the ticking of the clock. You can perhaps imagine how unnerving a severe-looking Amazon snipping away with a pair of scissors might've seemed to a first-grader, especially during an already anxious era of sonic booms, constant fire drills and full-on air raid practices, where we'd all have to scramble under our desks and duck and cover. (This bizarre ritual went on longer than many people believe.)

Crack was her yardstick that lived up on the chalk rail right underneath the little American flag. It was a good half an inch thick, made of wood the color of old ivory, with a fine rim of brass molded around the edges. I only saw her use it once to deliver a spanking (following a fight over the rubber cement) and it may have done Ronny Krieger some good, but it was a fearsome presence in the classroom, its name alone suggestive enough to cause a time-release alarm.

More often than not, her tantrums were purely vocal (although her eyes would both squint and bulge with disturbing effect). What was difficult to comprehend was their cause. They usually seemed unrelated to anything that had actually happened (and gradually they seemed to have more and more to do with me).

I think what fretted us kids more was her control over the use of the bathroom. Classes for kids that age usually had their own restrooms in the back (at least we did). It was a very big deal to raise your hand and ask to go. Maybe some kids did have some problems this way—and I can see how a teacher might not want the constant interruption of kid after kid getting up when a lesson was under way. Part of school at that age is just implanting a sense of routine and knowing when, like recess, to go to the bathroom. Mrs. Mauer didn't seem to feel that any time was appropriate and I think outright enjoyed watching us clamp our legs together. On more than a couple of occasions, accidents happened—and the humiliated culprit would have to clean up the mess in front of everyone. This did attract some parental concern—once. Belinda Thornwall (who was probably the most confident girl in the class) had been the unfortunate. Her parents made some inquiry into the incident—which I suspect Mrs. Mauer took grave exception to. The next afternoon, Belinda was asked to stay after class. There were no more parental intrusions after that.

I didn't have any mishaps with bodily functions. My problems with Mrs. Mauer were of a subtler and more sinister kind. At first they seemed harmless. I was even kind of proud. I was asked to go up to the board more often than any other child. And she'd always make a point of emphasizing my name, as if I'd just arrived in class that day. Gradually, the other kids began to pick up on this, over-pronouncing my name on the playground as a kind of taunt. It grew more and more irritating. One day I had to stay up at the board for what seemed like an eternity. Having all those eyes on me for so long made me feel like an animal in the zoo. I started to get flustered and began getting the answers wrong. The faces before me snickered and leered. I felt my face flush and thought I might cry. I wanted desperately to sit down. It was then that Mrs. Mauer began to actually make fun of me in front of the whole class. I sensed there was something wrong with this behavior, but I was too off-balance to bring my feelings into focus. I was afraid that my growing discomfort could escalate into the wide, black fear that would embarrass me utterly in plain sight of all.

So began a very disconcerting pattern of alternatingly being the teacher's pet and feeling like her whipping boy—without any understanding of what lay behind it. At first, when I told my parents what was happening, I don't think they grasped the seriousness of the situation. I didn't either, actually, and I was uncomfortable about sounding afraid, so I glossed over some of the important details. Not until she started insisting I stay after class almost each day did the relationship begin moving into shadowy terrain that would have a dramatic impact on me and reach a point that couldn't be ignored.

I remember very clearly the first afternoon she called me Donald. At first I thought I hadn't heard her right—or that she was confused—there wasn't any Donald in our class. But she repeated it and then a few moments later, she asked me directly, in a soft, wheedling sort of voice that brought barbs of sweat to my neck, "You don't mind me calling you Donald when no one else is around, do you?"

I, of course, did mind, although I didn't like it when she used my right name, either. And I very much didn't like her reminder of "no one else being around." It wasn't entirely true, of course, but she was canny enough to make it truer than I liked. She was beginning to not just worry me but to outright scare me. My digestion was affected. I was restless and troubled at night. During the day, my stomach always seemed to be churning with acid, my palms moist. I couldn't work out why I was being targeted or what I should do about it—and of course, the moment I showed any sign of panic, she'd instantly change mood and tactic and I'd once again be the hero of the class. Every day was a roller coaster ride. By now all of the other kids had picked up on how I was being treated, but perhaps because they didn't understand what was going on any better than I did, instead of taking my side and supporting me against her, they of course, being kids, just turned on me further. I started getting called a fairy by some of the other boys, which wounded me. I didn't comprehend what a fairy was, really—and yet I sort of did. Words that older kids used had started slipping in. It was part of the whole wind of the world my parents (at least my mother) wanted to keep out.

But if I've created the impression that Mrs. Mauer was only a harridan, I must add that she knew kids and was a skillful manipulator when it came to pleasing them as well as bullying. She knew what kinds of candy I liked (Reese's Peanut Butter Cups). She gave me a gyroscope. She had a clever way of playing to both my weaknesses and my strengths—and my greatest weakness was my private sense of my own strangeness. While I felt unfairly singled out, I also felt that in some secret way I deserved it. There was about our relationship an emerging unnatural intimacy that while alien, also seemed familiar to me, even though I couldn't say how.

Because the world seemed alive to me at every level, the Other World always peeking through, I was slow to pick up on a more obvious reason behind her behavior—the mundane and also random fact that out of all the boys in our class, I just happened to look the most like her dead son Donald. I remember the falling-through-the-floor feeling I had the day she brought in his photograph, and the resemblance clicked. Just like Snip.

He'd been hit by a car when he was about my age. How long ago that was she didn't say—or rather, she couldn't keep her story straight. Sometimes it was ten years ago. Other times her voice would get dreamy and her eyes would fog over and it was "last week." Believe it or not, I actually felt sorry for her—and she played on that too. So, when she brought in some of his old clothes for me to try on, the ghastly inappropriateness of the proceedings didn't worry me as much as it should have. Very gradually she'd drawn me into her delusion and I was finding it harder to get out.

I've since come to see that this is precisely how a certain kind of psychosis operates. The aggressor is adept at hiding aggression—especially from people outside the victim relationship. (Mrs. Mauer very cleverly managed to keep other teachers and staff away any time I was alone with her, and had set up an accepted scenario with the other students whereby I was both star pupil and class scapegoat.) Meanwhile the victim is made to feel more and more like an accomplice—and in fact partially becomes one. As the situation advances, it becomes harder for the victim to escape control. There's an underlying, destabilizing sense of shame and guilt (which makes the victim more vulnerable). It becomes ever more difficult to seek outside assistance, because the problem has been going on for a while—and the victim worries that the predator will be able to fool other people too well, so his story won't be believed. As long as the predator can keep the camouflage in place, the victim feels helpless, short of an overt confrontation, and this is of course the core fear that set the whole relationship in motion in the first place.

In the end, fear is the ultimate weapon. Once someone is afraid of you, you have them—and you can make them weaker still by making them grateful for your apparent kindness at strategic times. I did as Mrs. Mauer asked and tried on her dead son's clothes. After school, when the terrible bells in the hall were silent, I let her call me Donald. If I had to do a BM, she inspected my bottom to make sure I'd properly wiped myself. In return I was given candy Lucky Strike cigarettes, jelly bears, milk chocolate Liberty Bells, and plastic skulls full of fruit juice. Better still, she'd bring in marbles and an old skeleton key—then more exotic, magical things for my collection—things maybe Donald had owned . . . a midget Bible, the "size of a postage stamp," a U.S. Baby Tank . . . X-Ray Glasses, a mystic gypsy charm, serpent's eggs, sneezing powder and invisible ink, and something called the Little Giant—as the box said, "It's a microscope, an opera glass, a burning lens, a reading glass, a telescope, a compass, a pocket mirror all in one!" All of these treasures I kept safely hidden at home, like my fears. For it was fear that she was the best at—and in this campaign she and Donald had a formidable ally.

At the start of the year, the one bright, endearing presence in the classroom was a silly-looking but practical arithmetic aid that Miss Roscoe, the loopy art teacher, had made (she was a bit of an old beatnik). He was called the Counting King, a big plywood cartoon with red and gold robes, a goofy lopsided crown and a huge smile on his face. He had a tripod easel stand behind him to keep him propped up—and he came with a bunch of little blackbirds that you could attach to his arms as a means of learning about numbers (1's and 10's). We all liked the blackbirds.

Then one night, several classrooms got broken into (probably by some older kids), and the Counting King, along with Crack, the flag and the clock, were all taken. The King was eventually found but his arms had been broken off and his blackbirds were gone. We were all quite happy that Crack had disappeared, but sorry to have lost the King.

Well, two weeks later (which seemed a bizarre eternity to me), this cheerful guardian was replaced by an industrially made variation dubbed the Counting Clown. No doubt the manufacturers of this specimen were attempting to do exactly what Miss Roscoe had done—but despite the fun-sounding name—they couldn't have missed their mark more completely. The Counting Clown was made of a thin sheet of sharp white metal mounted on a rotating arm like a weathervane. They hadn't bothered to paint him, so he was pure silhouette, and being white gave him an odd blankness, like a hole cut into space. Where the King had had a funny crown, the Clown had a weird hat, somewhere between a derby and a top hat—with jagged suggestions of his hair shooting out from underneath—and what were supposed to be big floppy shoes. His head was turned in profile so you could see the line of the ball on his nose, but the angle had a kind of contorted look to it, as if his neck had been twisted. We all know that clowns can have a dark aspect at the best of times. But unpainted and seen only as an outline, this fellow was more threatening still—especially since he didn't come with fingers. Instead of the King's blackbirds, the counting function was achieved by attaching clothespins for his digits. He was thus often missing fingers, and when all were in position, he looked positively maniacal.

Mrs. Mauer wasn't immune to the anxiety this effigy created in us, and she was especially sensitive to how it upset me. So, whenever I didn't do a good-enough job cleaning the erasers—whenever I didn't stand up straight enough in her son's clothes, she'd say, "The Counting Clown doesn't always stay still in the classroom. At night he comes to life and he might come looking for you. You wouldn't want that to happen, would you?"

This was too much. I began having nightmares, not only about Donald, but about the Counting Clown. I could see and hear it creaking after me . . . standing in the streetlight shadows in front of our house, waiting for me . . . calling to me in its faceless, clothespin-fingered voice. The presence of Donald, Mrs. Mauer's car-mangled dead son, and the Counting Clown took root in my dreams. I became withdrawn and different at home in ways I couldn't control. One night at dinner when my mother was there (she often wasn't because of work), I blurted out that Mrs. Mauer wanted to take me away on a weekend trip to visit some of our old relatives. My mother dropped her fork and said, "Whose relatives?"

To her credit, she barged into principal Mrs. Day's office, the next morning. (I strangely have no recollection of my father's involvement with the issue whatsoever—a theme that would repeat.) Mom was late for work at her own school and furious. The whole thing came out then.

Actually, the whole thing didn't come out, because there were still elements of my relationship with Mrs. Mauer that I didn't understand fully enough to explain or, where I did, felt willing to repeat. All that was needed was a mention of her dead son's clothes and the wanting to take me away for a weekend, and ever-practical Principal Day stepped in. Fast.

What happened to Mrs. Mauer I don't know. There were rumors that some men came for her that afternoon. Like Ichabod Crane, she was never seen again, and Mrs. Day personally took over the running of our class for the rest of the year. Still, the Counting Clown remained in position, and in my dreams he'd walk stiffly down the streets at night, a harbinger of darkness. And Donald? Dead boys aren't so easily evaded.

"Why do you always check the sheets before you climb into bed?" my sister asked one night.

I thought it best not to tell her I was looking for the blood.

I'D SHOW THEM ALL

I had to have a secret thought for every day and I'd whisper certain words and phrases over and over to myself. I always had to have a pencil or a pen or something in my hand and I'd trace figure eights in the air very fast, or I'd pretend the pen was a runner sprinting down the football field.

There were endless sporting highlights—scorching the hundred-meter dash in the Olympics, scoring thousands of touchdowns, smashing a grand slam in the bottom of the ninth in the tie-breaker game of the World Series, hitting a twenty-five-foot jump shot at the buzzer to win the NBA finals, slamming consecutive ace serves at Wimbledon. Knockout punches and board-splitting karate chops.

I had this ongoing fantasy that I was going to disappear into some magical world like Narnia or Middle Earth, or aliens from another galaxy were going to take me away. I'd be gone for only an hour of Earth time but I'd have lived and learned for centuries. I'd come back and I'd have read every book.

I made lists of all the subjects I was going to devour, the words I'd learn, the places I'd travel to. I'd have secret weapons the aliens gave me, or things I stole, like Jack nabbing the goose from the giant and racing down the beanstalk. I'd be able to shrink bullies with an evil glance and put them inside rat cages where they'd learn their lesson and beg to be released. I was always giving interviews in my head and writing down the names of the outfielders and investigative reporters I was going to be when I finished flying twin-engine Otters into blizzards, discovering lost cities, occasionally racing stock cars and becoming the world's foremost authority on the criminal mind.

JUMP WITH ME

The highlight of my partnership with my sister, driven by our enslaved devotion to Van Cheese, was Halloween (one of the loveliest smells I know is that first stringy spoonful of moist pumpkin seed goop coming out of a jack-o'-lantern and being dumped onto newspaper). Brainstorming about costumes would begin as early as August, with my sister aiming to have drawings and a review of logistics well in hand come Labor Day. In successive years we dominated the school parade awards for best costumes, appearing as court jesters, robots, and alternative superheroes like Rat Man and the Bee. Aunt Mabo was called in as master seamstress. Mom and Gaja assisted with makeup. We had quite a bit of involvement with pipe cleaners, spray paint, cardboard boxes and old bedsheets.

My sister broke new ground with our final joint appearance (and it was a very sad night the last time we went out trick-or-treating together; many things would never be the same). We went as germs. Yep. Like bacteria. It was a stroke of brilliance. She got the idea from some little cartoon drawings in the *World Book*—but it was very lateral for the time and made all the pirates and fairy princesses seem obvious and bland. We painted white sheets with disgusting colors and sewed paper cones suggesting spikes of ugly hairs to them—along with squiggles of wire. It was messy and genuinely scary, but playful too. Everyone was quite surprised and the refrain of the evening sums up what many people thought of her then: "Now where does she get her ideas?"

She had a special genius for covert operations. When the McMurtrys, a prunish older couple down the street, stiffed her for payment in a peanut brittle fund-raising drive, we vowed massive retaliation. The McMurtrys hated Halloween and would do anything to be away from the house on that night, except they were stingy. So my sister, with some old stationery and my mother's typewriter, agonizingly crafted a plausible enough letter informing the M's that they had won a "Special Halloween Weekend" package at a motel down in Carmel, with a FREE all-you-can-eat buffet and early check-in. She included a little map of the area our mother had saved—and a branded complimentary chocolate—and sent the envelope to them special delivery to get around the postmark problem.

Then to my astonishment, she actually pulled off a confirmation phone call to them with a suspiciously well-disguised voice. She was a terrier for detail. Halloween was on a Friday that year, and sure enough, the McMurtrys loaded up in the late morning to get down for "early check-in." We, meanwhile, had skipped school, which was a sacrifice, as I (gone solo now) was defending champion in the costume parade and a shoe-in to retain the title. But we had other things on our minds—like breaking in to the McMurtrys and decorating for the huge Haunted House Halloween Party, to which every kid we knew, even those we hated (especially those we hated), were invited. We'd made flyers and gotten them printed using our slush fund. Friends were passing them out at school. We posted some in the library and the post office. If our victims hadn't fallen for it, I don't know what we would've done, but my sister had a cool head when it came to these types of things—and had the smarts to take the phone off the hook. The McMurtrys had a lot of parents fooled about their hatred of kids, so most people didn't question it. Some did call, though, we found out later, and when they got a busy signal, they just thought, "Oh, well, there are probably a lot of people wondering about the party."

But here's the reason why, even at twelve, my sister could've run the CIA. In case any parents physically stopped by the house to check things out, we'd coerced a friend of our dad's and his girlfriend, who we had some dirt on, to drift around the house with sheets over their heads, acting like ghosts. Everyone thought they were the McMurtrys. (Access to the McMurtrys' liquor cabinet greatly assisted with this crucial element, we later found out.) Late that afternoon, when some pressure was applied, and all through evening, when the goblins and Tin Men started showing up, if anyone asked, "Where are the McMurtrys?" my sister and I would just say, "Oh, they're ghosts . . . haunting the house."

"Isn't that lovely," our mother said. "They're really getting into the spirit of things."

Meanwhile, just as she'd predicted, once the McMurtrys got all the way down to Carmel, they weren't going to turn around and come home on Halloween. No, they stayed away while God's own Haunted House Party raged—kids spewing in the bathroom, jack-o'-lantern cake smeared on the walls, Hershey's Kisses crushed underfoot. We'd put down sheets to protect the furniture (and to add to the spooky ambience) but it was more or less total devastation from prunish older people's points of view.

Best of all, we'd made a whole group of parents, who were just glad the festivities weren't happening at their house, accomplices in the crime. When the shit hit the fan, and it did, we had a lot of shoulders to offload responsibility on. I'm only sorry my sister later went straight. She was the real deal when it came to the big con and could've conducted a mean briefing in the Situation Room.

It was a tough thing to lose that sense of partnership and collusion. Growing older will do that—we all move rather too easily from parent permission slips to promissory notes, without knowing how or why. Still, I think of her now and I see her with her sewing machine, paints and plans—or practicing the famous speech for class president in junior high, which ended with the rather too-memorable pep rally slogan, "Don't be a slug stuck in the mire, jump with me, go higher and higher!"

I practiced that jump with her . . . not knowing how high I'd get one day or how far away I'd land.

LORD OF LORDS

Before he lost his faith in the church and became a kind of crackpot psychologist, my father was quite an inspiring preacher—although he had a humorous knack of confusing words at dramatic moments in such a way as "to bring the house down," as my choir director mother put it.

He could, for instance, raise his arms in that gentle entreating way of his and request that the congregation all stand . . . "Please rise now and turn to face the person next to you . . . and give them the Piss of Keace." (His "splash" of gin prior to each service may have had some influence on this tendency. I certainly always relished it when he would say things like, or try to say things like, "the Apocrypha and the Pseudepigrapha," after his third splash. I didn't know what he was talking about then, but it made me giggle.)

More than once he bewildered his attentive listeners with such variations on accepted wisdom as, "It's easier for a rich man to go through the eye of a needle than it is for a camel to enter the kingdom of God." (Once, the needle ended up in the camel's eye, and another time, there were rich men searching for needles in heaven.) Despite some celebrated gaffes that caused an uproar of laughter, many slid by the majority of churchgoers only to end up in circulation around the Sunday afternoon dinner table, which invariably caused my father to spill gravy on his tie—such was his mixture of chagrin, disbelief and chuckling enjoyment at his own misstatements. You could never fault him for not being able to laugh at himself. As much as he loathed and shrunk and wilted at the slightest hint of a barbed criticism, if anything was ever funny, he'd laugh.

To his further credit, it must be said that he did excellent, heartfelt weddings and his Easter services were always exceptionally meaningful. There were clearly some key aspects of Christian theology that were at odds with his personal beliefs and anything along the lines of harping on doing good grated on him—but he could blow the hell out of a theme like the Resurrection and the Life. One could easily imagine the stained-glass windows coming to life on Easter Sunday.

My mother adopted a kind of player-coach role in the choir, often taking the solos for soprano (and sometimes for alto too). Although she could be abrasive, she always raised the standard. People kept in time and in tune, and if by some odd chance my father took to rambling, she had sufficient control of her team and music generally to be able to spontaneously introduce a piece that wasn't listed on the hymn board. The songs never rocked as in a black Baptist church, but they occasionally soared and they never once sank or stank. (It would be impossible to count the number of thoroughly average people over the years my mother taught how to "*dee-liver* the message.")

My father had no musical training whatsoever and not a clue about the volume and strength of his own voice (which could easily overwhelm the entire front row on even a packed morning)—and he often seemed to take a competitive stance toward the choir. Fortunately, he was gifted with a naturally pleasing voice, resonant and committed, with none of the "slushing and slurring" that so infuriated my mother in most others. At their best, they were a true President and First Lady partnership, and they were at their best when they were in partnership. Church was the family business and they were unquestionably good at it.

Which isn't to say they didn't have some considerable failures—of a relatively spectacular nature, given the context. I was involved in perhaps the biggest one, although I'm exceedingly relieved to say I wasn't the weak leak in the chain. That role fell to little Grace Kenneally.

If you know anything about the Protestant racket, you'll appreciate the savor of winning back some Catholics, and the Kenneallys were a big Catholic family (just like the Gages, who lived next door to us). Mr. Kenneally, whatever his first name was, was in retail and on the rise commercially. I don't know what it was he sold, but it had something to do with housewares and he had a vast warehouse down on San Pablo and was always passing out business cards and making fine tactical use of the after-service coffee time to shake hands and pass out ever more cards (I always wondered where he kept them all). His wife looked continuously exhausted, as perhaps a mother of six well might—but she was extremely proud of her brood and her tight, clenched face would overly relax into a soft, doughy mass when any compliments on their dress or demeanor came her way. (I got brushed and mussed and primped each Sunday myself, but I think those kids got a full military inspection.)

Gracie was the bright light in the bunch. Horace was her twin (who in their right mind would name a child Horace?). They were my age. Sadly, Horace had a speech impediment, so when it came time to assign roles for the young children's contribution to the annual Christmas pageant, my mother made the decision to feature Grace, as a gesture of compensation to the image-conscious Kenneallys. It took a great deal of restraint on her part not to force the starring role on me, but she knew the game and what was at stake. Mr. Kenneally placed real folding money in the collection trays that went around each service—and did so with great ceremony. Horace was hopeless at speaking a word in public; Grace got the nod. An understandable move.

It was my father who insisted that the pageant not be an isolated event in the Sunday school, but that instead, it be brought right into the main service for all to see. Let the little children come unto me. *Truly I say to you, whoever does not receive the kingdom of God like a child will not enter it at all.* Luke 18:17.

So, in my mother's practiced wisdom, we practiced. We rehearsed our little asses off—for three full weeks. I had a line about the Wise Men following the star. Gracie had five lines . . . including the big finale. It was a call-and-response deal that Mom wrote herself. Dad would say, "And who is Christ?" . . . and Grace would answer, "He's Lord of Lords and King of Kings." Easy.

I don't know how many times we went over that. It seemed endless. And poor Grace was forced by her earnest socialite mother to be forever repeating that grand end line even when we weren't in rehearsal. One would've thought the child was going bonkers the way she was always mouthing it to herself and to those of us sentenced to the same Sunday school—where there was always much talk of the Lamb of God and the Lamb lying down with the Lion—and then lamb served at the dinner table only a couple of hours later.

Well, not surprisingly, the sanctuary was full to fire regulation limits on the day in question. My parents didn't mess around when it came to drumming up a crowd—or rather a congregation. My father even went as far as to initiate a *free* pancake breakfast on the same day, as a lure to the street people, who were beginning to show distinct signs of an increase in numbers. There was going to be no question that the Christmas pageant would be well attended, slackers or not.

Every inch of every pew was crammed with flesh, however willing, whatever way their spirits were inclined. I've never smelled so much perfume and cologne in my life—which was a good thing as some of the park sleepers who took up the back rows more than balanced the equation, with body odor, felt, weary old denim, scabies skin and maple syrup.

It started out rough, when my father asked the assembled children, "Whose birthday are we celebrating today?" Billy Piper was quick to raise his hand and announce, "Mine!"

That got everyone snickering and threw off the timing of the recitals, but my mother icily reined us all back in. Slowly we made our way through the script, as the congregation shuffled patiently in the pews, eyes wide and hopeful that we'd pull off our respective parts.

And we did. We dee-livered the message, as my mother would say. I got my star over the manger. Young Horace, somewhat thick of tongue and thicker of mind, managed to raise his branch of holly at the correct moment. Gracie shone. In fact, we got some black rouse out of a mainly white house . . . until . . . until the grand finale.

I looked over at my father, thankful I hadn't messed up my line, knowing that he was ever mindful of my mother, watching over all of us like the proverbial hawk. One step away from total success. One simple question in what he could make sound like a big, booming voice. One simple answer from Gracie—and we'd be done. We'd have blistered it. Applause in church, which is unusual for white people. We'd be heroes—or at least have passed muster in my mother's eyes—one step away from the covered part of the church courtyard and the remains of the pancake breakfast anyway.

So, my father stepped theatrically forward, right on cue, steady as he goes (it was definitely but a one-splash morning). "And who is Christ?"

Cue to Gracie . . .

The whole congregation, even the street people, who were a little rowdy and unused to the stained-glass and organ ritual, went stone still.

Grace, who'd done so well up to this point, suddenly paused. Her face froze over with an expression of pure terror. She'd forgotten the line. Gone.

There was a moment of awkward silence verging on pain . . . and then people started shifting and murmuring. Jesus, that sound can only be so loud in church.

My father, ever the optimist, didn't grasp the nature of the crisis. He didn't realize Gracie's mind had gone completely blank. He thought it was just an opportunity to enhance the theater of the performance. He tried again . . .

"And WHO is Christ?"

"He's Lord of Lords . . . and . . . "

And? And? *And . . . ?*

Gracie just didn't have the line—the final line. The closer! The cue for the organist and the choir. Everything was stopped. Stalled. Dead in the water. The street people were getting restless.

I watched my father peer over quickly at my mother, looming before her robed choir. It was beginning to dawn on him how serious the situation was. The Kenneallys (the entire clan other than Grace and Horace) were in the front row—and they were *squirming* with anxiety of the purest kind. Mr. Kenneally's face had clouded over so darkly it looked like he'd never pass out another business card again. Mrs. Kenneally looked so clenched it seemed like she'd never pass water again. And one of the more degenerate street people my father, in his enthusiasm for the event, had invited in to witness the celebration of Christ's birth, was mumbling something about "Lord of the Bored" back near the doors.

My mother gave Dad one of her most piercing glances, as if to say, "This is all your fault—you never should've let those people in here."

Of course it was too late to worry about that, and my father was never one to worry about a bad decision anyway—things would work out. He'd just try the line again.

And so he did. Same response. No response. Worse response! One of the ushers actually laughed. I heard my mother clear her throat (never a good sign). The fuse had been lit. She was fuming! She was about to cue the organist. She was about to unleash the choir to cover the debacle. The pageant was in disarray. There'd be hell to pay for this. Disaster. Apocalypse!

And then . . . *and then* . . .

Then I saw a glimmer of illumination in Gracie's eyes. The penny had dropped. She'd recovered. The horror was past. Her stage fright had evaporated. She'd remembered the words. She was going to pull the line and all of us out of the fire. She was back in time and in tune, and she was going to proudly let it rip with all her heart. My mother always said, "If you can say it—and you *will* say it—then sing it out! Make people sit up and take notice. This is not about being an eeny weeny quiet little mouse—this is about making the people in the back row know you're alive!"

Gracie gave a slight but confident nod to my father. *Cue me again. Have faith in me.* She nodded to my father, who had faith in scabbed people scratching themselves audibly. She put it right back onto him, the one person in that whole high-ceilinged room who would never have gotten into a fight but who would never, *ever* have knocked back any dare if it came to a matter of faith and a possible good outcome. My father knew he'd been challenged where he lived—and he stepped right in close and dee-livered that cue line as if he'd never said it before . . .

"Tell me, Grace, who is Christ?"

"He's Lord of Lords!" Gracie belted out.

"Yes?" my father interjected for theatrical effect. "Yes . . . ?"

Gracie screwed up her pretty little face and literally bellowed . . . *"And . . . HE'S KING OF THE JUNGLE!"*

Faster than you can blink, my mother flagged her arm and commanded the organist and her choir to hit it—the Hallelujah Chorus at full bore. But not even that onslaught of music could drown out the laughter or the awful mechanical and pastry settling sound of the retraction of the Kenneallys' egos. It couldn't even outdo my father's own hilarity. He buckled over double in his shiny ministerial robe and just plain guffawed in weeping gratitude for this new insight on the nature of Christ Our Lord. He chortled. He whinnied. He held nothing back. I tell you, if it was funny, my father laughed and you did too. And if it was very funny, then he gave birth to some new emotion, right in front of you.

"I knew it!" one of the homeless men shouted with Old Testament conviction and then proceeded to give a spirited *roar* for the Christ child. My mother did her best to lift the decibel level of the choir, but she couldn't match the lion's roar—or the further explosion of mirth it triggered in my father. I doubt seriously if any church has ever shaken with so much joyful noise. People were physically clutching their stomachs trying to contain themselves.

What followed was decidedly different. The Kenneallys made it through the after-service Christmas party with a grim, stoic calm (without Mr. Kenneally passing out a single business card). They were never seen in church again, which is a sad ending to the story, for little Gracie had done exactly as my mother had instructed. Plus, King of the Jungle has a nice ring to it—and very possibly a lot more Christmas spirit than King of Kings, which to my ears sounded a bit too much like one of Mr. Kenneally's ad slogans.

To make matters even more pointed, my father mistakenly tried to sum up the proceedings and smooth things over once we were back at home and seated at dinner, by remarking as philosophically as he could sound, "Well, you know what they say about show business. Never work with kids or children."

To which my mother replied with a frosted glare, "The line is, never work with kids or *animals*, dear."

Of course that only got my sister and me started once more. I think it's safe to say the gravy fairly flew that day.

For years after, the very softest suggestion of anything even vaguely like "King of the Jungle" would bring up my father's belly laugh, tears streaming down his face. From that day forth, we were never without a means to cheer ourselves up at short notice. And as it turns out, we'd damn well need it.

HEAT LIGHTNING

We trapped fireflies at dusk in what my aunt with the palsy called relaxing jars, and cheered when Tarzan killed a giant spider on the white sheet stretched between two trees, the heat lightning flickering for miles beyond the town's big water tower.

All summer long I lay awake with cousins I was never going to see again, whispering and listening to Motown music, pressed against the cool bricks in the basement that smelled like the lawn mower and the pumice soap my uncle used after changing oil.

My uncle was famous for rescuing a drowning boy without even dropping his pipe, then killing a woman a week to the day later on a golf course. He hooked his drive and hit her hard in the temple and she keeled over in front of the clubhouse, dead. It's true, I swear to God.

Every night, he'd poke his head down the stairs to see if we were asleep and my cousin would have to twist in bed to silence the radio. Then we'd hold our breath for what seemed like the whole summer until we heard the footsteps fading away.

On my last night, we let all our fireflies free in the basement, so we'd have our own lightning, and we stayed awake till dawn, making promises—wondering what was going to happen to us next summer, and the next summer, and the summer after that.

JOSEPH COTTEN

For years I lived in fear of the monster that I believed emerged from a pond in the movie Hush, Hush, Sweet Charlotte. I could hear the eerie song echoing in my head from some movie preview . . . visions and memory scent of the Grand Lake theater in Oakland or the Oaks in Berkeley . . . scenes and shadows seemingly cast on the cavernous walls of Larry Blake's restaurant, where everyone in the family ate salad but me. I see the old decaying house and the long spiraling staircase from the monster's point of view as it climbs the steps, dripping leaves and mud . . . some awful shape of nightmare curiosity . . .

When I finally saw the movie all the way through many years later, I realized it wasn't a pond, but a creek, and the monstrous shape I'd been imagining all that time was really Joseph Cotten. He and the crooked Olivia de Havilland are trying to drive Bette Davis mad. What I'd been seeing in my mind and dreams was a supposedly drowned Joseph Cotten come back from the dead.

Flashback to a summer night in Tahoe . . .

My father's friend Bill with the deep, smoky voice . . . his ballerina wife and their two children, Wade and Wendy, are there. Bill is going bald and his skin has a stained, leathery look like something left too long in the sun. He has liver spots. The wife's hair is pulled back tight into a bun, her body is slender and petite, her face vaguely Spanish-looking. My mother never knows what to say to her unless they're beating the men at bridge. She dislikes them because Bill and Dad slip off to Stateline or Reno and gamble all night. Bill plays black-jack and has won as much as $5,000 in a weekend. Wade is a weird kid and Wendy wets her pants and cries. We go to the movies. The drive-in in South Lake Tahoe. (My God, there are still drive-ins.) A Hammer horror film is showing, *The Mummy's Shroud*. I cover my eyes throughout, only glimpsing up at the most terrifying moments, which two decades later I realize are actually quite ludicrous. It's a hot, dark August night full of bugs thick like fog in the light, and far outside the glow of the giant screen and the cinderblock snack bar, the stars are trembling.

I see now that it's Bill I'm really afraid of. But back there in the car before the shining screen, I don't know why. I only sense it. A darkness taking shape. I think what I'm afraid of is his deep, smoky voice and the curling lip of his laugh that I never know how to take—and the way he always says my mother's name as if it's a question. It's not the colors of the movie that I close my eyes to hear . . . it's the way he wants me to look, the way he likes that I'm afraid. The way he eats his Junior Mints with methodical calm.

Wade whispers about penises and ladies' things. Wendy sobs softly and the stars dissolve over the Sierras. The smell of popcorn and steamed hot-dog buns fills the car and for years I'll be afraid of a bad movie, not knowing why.

MAD MOUSE

Fourth of July. Our pink napkins stick to the crystals of salt on the clammy baked ham. We're surrounded by stuffed basset hounds and battery-operated back scratchers. "Not for the fainthearted," the man who plays the killer ape in the Haunted Trailer tells me. Call it a mine car, call it a midget roller coaster—the name of the ride is the Mad Mouse.

Two by two the passengers return, dazed by dizziness, still screaming for the dreaming crowd. Then the Mad Mouse begins to chug and grind again. Two fresh pilots without wheels to steer. A girl behind her gawky boyfriend catches my eye.

I watch her grip the guardrail as they head into the first furious turn. I reach for something to hold, too. My body tenses in time with hers—but I'm a believer in the inherent stinginess of carnivals. Her ride will be over all too soon.

Who could've foreseen the car derailing, launched like Fireball XL5 through the thin lattice of the trellis surrounding the track? Off she went, alone after impact. Destination . . . the solitary white booth that sold Polar Mist.

She looks down at the corn dogs, the iron milk bottles and the dishes of dimes. And me. I think she's singing, until I recognize the scream. Blue slush dripping down the splintered plywood.

My sister had the sense to drag me away. But every summer for years to come, I'd see that girl in her crazy convertible without a wheel, wailing over the livestock and the whirligigs, on her way to the most magnetic of the poles. I'd hear her voice, thinking she was trying to tell me something.

BAD HOMBRE

My sister made stuff and made stuff happen, as I've said.

Like a stuffed mouse for one of our younger cousins, Dennis. She made it out of a soft gray terrycloth towel filled with cotton batting. It had big ears lined with white pillowcase cutouts, black button eyes, a long nose with a black velvet tip, a black satin bow tie, and a red-and-white striped vest that came from an off-cut of the fabric from her bedroom curtains. It looked like a barbershop quartet mouse. She gave it to Dennis for his third birthday, when it seemed like the mouse was bigger than he was.

Dennis took to the toy instantly. Actually, it was kind of creepy from the start, the way he hugged the thing so tightly—the way he identified with it so *intensely*—as if my sister had put her finger right on the great need in his life. A soft, cuddly friend who would never refuse his affection.

Dennis was one of those shrimpy kids you could tell would one day (probably overnight) turn into a giant. Until that moment, though, he'd be undersized—in all ways. He was desperate for recognition, prone to tantrums and forever ignored by his father, a tall, bald man who enjoyed raking leaves. His mother (our mother's sister), once a highly competent woman with a promising career at Procter

& Gamble, chose motherhood and small town community leadership over corporate success. She became a champion in the strawberry shortcake and macaroni salad league. Dennis's sister, Amelia, was my age and got all the parental attention. She played the cello from a very young age (and looked like a cello). Dennis was a breathless asthmatic runt who couldn't compete. The mouse was just what he needed. My sister was very pleased with her creation.

Dennis named the mouse Gus Gus and carried it with him everywhere during our visit. Then we went home, back to California, and thought no more of it.

The next summer, however, we saw them again—and we *met* Gus Gus. The mouse was a little worse for wear, or love. The clean white insides of the ears had soiled, the velvet-tipped nose had been rubbed dull, and the red-and-white striped vest showed signs of fraying (we found out later that Amelia had tossed the mouse in a mud puddle in the spring), but generally speaking, the creature was holding up pretty well—considering that Dennis carried it with him wherever he went. This gratified my sister. At first.

What took us all by surprise was the fact that Gus Gus now talked—in a high-pitched sleepy voice that was a little unnerving to hear. After a short while, it got really annoying. What was more surprising still (and I think you'd have to say outright disturbing) was that Dennis didn't talk. Not anymore. Not to other people, anyway. He'd speak to Gus Gus, but when it came to communicating with anyone else, Gus Gus did his talking for him.

Even our mother found this a trifle odd, and yet she went along with it, because it seemed like their family had given in and accepted this relationship as normal. Basically, if you wanted to talk to Dennis, you had to talk to the mouse. The added curiosity was that when you did start talking to Gus Gus, you found yourself starting to talk *like* Gus Gus.

I could tell my sister was beginning to have doubts about the gift. But always a great rationalizer, my mother said to us privately, "Oh, well, he'll grow out of it. The magic of childhood ends so soon." This struck my sister and me as a very strange remark, given that we weren't much older. I'd had this knitted cotton hat that I liked the smell of and kept with me all the time for comfort, and everyone had made a big deal of weaning me off it. But I didn't talk to it! And it certainly didn't talk for me. And I didn't take photographs of it on family outings.

Dennis had pictures of Gus Gus at Niagara Falls, on the steps of the state capitol, sitting in a wheelbarrow full of apples—even out in front of Radio City Music Hall when they'd gone down to the city for Amelia's cello competition. Here I thought I was running strong in the odd-kid sweepstakes. My little cousin was in a class of his own.

Our father found the whole thing "case-study material" (which, given some of his own tendencies, was a bit rich), but my sister and I remained open-minded. As long as Gus Gus didn't start walking around on his own in the night, or wasn't blamed for any mischief that Dennis got up to, we thought the phase would pass.

Come the next summer, when they came out west to visit us, we had to revise our opinion. Gus Gus was starting to look seriously battered by this point. He'd lost a button eye. The worn bow tie gave the impression the mouse had tried to hang himself. The striped vest was filthy and slit with holes and tears—and the stuffed beast stank like an old pillow. My sister couldn't help but wonder if she'd done the right thing with this well-intentioned creation.

More importantly, Gus Gus was still doing Dennis's talking. My father found this somewhere between highly amusing and totally astonishing, and you could tell he wanted to make notes (any indication of eccentricity in my mother's family was a source of profound delight and relief for him).

My mother was *not* amused in the least. This was a situation that could no longer be ignored—and yet that's exactly what Dennis's parents did. They had completely accepted Gus Gus as a member of their family. Even Amelia. This rotting stuffed mouse that looked like a dog had gotten to it (which was in fact true) was still being photographed on the family's travels. The helium voice was still the ventriloquist dummy for Dennis (or maybe it was the other way around).

We were to find out over the course of their time with us that Amelia had, in a moment of insufferable irritation, buried the mouse in the back garden. Dennis simply dug his friend up—after all, who was going to talk for him, if not Gus Gus? Dennis's father confessed to my father late one night that he'd contemplated plopping the mouse on top of a pile of burning leaves (how many people seriously enjoy raking leaves and have a special plaid shirt they only wear when doing it?), but after the exhumation, he was concerned that the destruction of the creature might cause "psychological harm." Boy, did Dad's ears prick up at that.

My mother was infuriated at the reflection on her breeding, but couldn't say anything, because her sister had recently won a first prize for her potato salad and made all our lunches. Aunt Orpha took the optimistic view that the mouse would one day have to fall apart in Dennis's hands and then the crisis would be passed. The inevitable disintegration strategy. Besides, it was my sister who'd started the whole thing.

I must say this for my older sis, she was never one to shrink from responsibility (at least not until she started manifesting signs of her own issues). The matter came to a head, so to speak, when we made a joint family pilgrimage to Virginia City, Nevada.

The town's motto is "Step Back in Time," and whenever you hear words like that, you need to be on your guard, because translated, they mean, "Give Us Your Money." To be fair, the town does have some real history, and some of it is intact (old churches, restored mansions, saloons and mine shafts from the gold and silver days of the Comstock Lode). But the plinky-plink player piano music coming out of the fake dancehalls starts to get to you. The plank boardwalks seem suspiciously new, the cigar store Indians too well varnished—and how many mentions of Mark Twain do you want within fifty feet?

This was once the wild and woolly mineral strike town made famous by the Bonanza kings, who shipped in crystal chandeliers, gilt, brass, oriental carpets and Renaissance artwork from San Francisco, Chicago and Denver. What it was when we passed through, and what it is still, is a whole lot of expensive Western kitsch. T-shirts, ice cream, cowboy hats, rubber rattlesnakes, replica bullets, gold nuggets—any kind of souvenir you can name—from beer coasters to mining tins. Come see the old-timer who tells tales of shoot-outs on the main street. Take a stagecoach ride! And of course, since it's Nevada, there's a chance for the adults to gamble, while the kids are sucking down fizzy drinks or learning how to lasso a fencepost.

What my sister saw in this extravaganza of pioneer bad taste was an opportunity to separate Dennis from Gus Gus in a seemingly authentic way (authenticity being the theme of the town). It happened while we were in line for the stagecoach, watching a grizzled man in costume trying to get a burro that was sitting down to stand up (I thought it not entirely impossible that the burro was in costume too). Dennis and Gus Gus went off to the restrooms with Aunt Orpha.

My sister and I had each been given a small stash of rubber

rattlesnake money, and she knew just what she was going to do with hers. She targeted this rowdy boy fooling around behind us—and she paid him off. He was an older fat kid who looked like he'd kill his own mother for another hot dog. He wasn't hard to convince. All he had to do was wait until Dennis returned, then yank Gus Gus from his hands. Dennis would naturally resist this with all the inner strength of his damaged personality. My sister figured Gus Gus wouldn't hold up to the tug-of-war and would split apart at the seams, never to be pieced together. Fat Boy would run off into the crowd, and we'd all be in the clear. There'd be no one really to blame and Dennis would just have to move on.

My sister was very good with instructions (plus she added that she'd put an Eskimo Pie down Fat Boy's underwear if he blew it). He pulled off his assignment all right. It all went precisely according to her plan. Dennis regained his place in line, clutching the foul-smelling mouse—Fat Boy made his move, with a few opening taunts to get Dennis braced for conflict . . .

"Hey, let me see that thing! This your little friend? Let me have a look, pip-squeak."

Wow. The sound Gus Gus made ripping apart. It was as if something inside Dennis had torn asunder. Cotton batting exploded, the striped vest ripped—and the head came right off. Fat Boy did just as he'd been briefed, and no doubt ran off to get his chili dog with extra fried onions. We assumed our best expressions of shock. Aunt Orpha reached for her kidney tablets (and probably a few aspirin too). Dennis went ballistic. Hysterical. It was all I could do to hold him back from running after Fat Boy, but at least he was too upset to see the setup. Tough love.

And a tough time for the other folks on the stagecoach ride, with Dennis squealing and screaming the whole way around the town, as if someone had put a scorpion down his checked shorts. But any kid, even Dennis, can only cry and bellow so much. Eventually, he exhausted himself as much as everybody else, and just sobbed and hiccupped. I think he'd wet his pants in the commotion (that boy went to the toilet more than you can believe). He had to stand in the sun, and a root beer float helped calm him further. I don't think the stagecoach people were too happy, but they'd seen kids crap their pants and upchuck before.

All might've gone just as my sister had planned, if I hadn't gotten what I thought was a funny idea. I don't know what snuck into me. Maybe it was the bizarreness of the situation that had gone uncommented on for so long. In any case, while we were all strolling around trying to recover from the "incident," and wondering if Dennis would ever talk to us again (as himself), I got distracted by two Mark Twain look-alikes having a dispute about who had rights to a particular corner, and I fell behind. Then I chanced to look down, and I spied Gus Gus's head lying in the dust below the boardwalk. Fat Boy must've thrown it there.

Well, right out in front was a concession that took a photograph of you and turned it into your very own genuine wanted poster, on fancy faded paper, no less. I hadn't spent my tourist trap money. I had just enough. And no one was looking for me yet. It's hard to get lost for long in a town like that. The wording was all set, so all I had to do was hand the photographer the ravaged head of the stuffed toy mouse—and they did the rest.

WANTED

$500 for this Bad Hombre, a bold Bandito
and Cold-Blooded Killer, Horse Thief, Cattle Rustler,
Claim Jumper, and all-around Notorious Character

No questions asked. All they wanted was the money, and that was it. Within about five minutes, I had a full-fledged wanted poster featuring a dirty, one-eyed, shredded stuffed-animal head. Gus Gus actually did look like a bad hombre. I felt very proud. Then I chucked the head in one of the fake horse troughs, just in case Dennis had any ideas about pleading for some kind of repair surgery. Of course, when I caught up to the family again, I couldn't resist showing him the poster. I knew it was wrong (and my sister later shoved an Eskimo Pie down my pants so that I was sure). I'd put her whole scheme at risk . . . but I just couldn't help myself. I had to see the look on Dennis's face. Gus Gus really did look like a bandito—if there ever was one. I tried to make out that Fat Boy had made the poster, which I'd just happened to find and that I'd never seen the head, but I don't think anyone believed me. And no one really cared, not even Dennis, because he'd gone off to some other place in his mind.

That trip back to Reno has to be the longest, most painful drive on record for a family vacation. It was hot enough by that point to fry both eggs and bacon on the hood of the car, everyone stuffed in so tight we couldn't move, sweaty and grumpy and sick from the food—and for all my sister's careful engineering, Gus Gus was still with us, only now his voice was a little lower and he kept saying, "I'm a cold-blooded killer . . . I'm a cold-blooded killer." The packed-out Rambler would get so quiet then, I could hear my father making mental notes.

NO PRISONERS

A *cold blue dawn on the banks of the Tuolumne River.* I'm snuggled in an old sleeping bag with a soft flannel lining that has pictures of deer and moose on it. It smells of sleep and smoke and pine needles, and the canvas of the tent is still cool from the damp.

The old man has taken me along with Dave, my godfather with the close-cropped hair and the big, pointy nose he plays like a Jew's harp when he's had enough to drink. My father is already back from fishing. He's whistling softly so I know he didn't get skunked. He must've risen before the moon set. I rub the sleep out of my eyes and see him crouched against the lonely blue-streaked sky in the west. The east is going gold and his face is braced against the light, his boulder-shadowed body huge behind him. Then he begins to move.

I imagine he's slicing the slick belly of the trout he's just caught straight down the middle, with his bone-handled jack-knife. He'll bury the guts. Soon the fry pan will be spitting and the smell of trout will cloud around the tent, calling me out. I sniff for the bitter, reassuringly adult smell of his campsite coffee, brewed up in a can the way he imagines cowboys did it, hunkered down under the stars, hearing the coyotes howl. Then I fall back asleep, smelling, listening.

Rattle of pans, splash of water and stinging smoke of a white ash fire. The sun is hot now. It's cleanup time. He tried to rouse me but I was dreaming and didn't wake up. Dad's bent over, washing up with his back turned, jawing happily, telling my godfather jokes.

He tells the one about the three-legged man, which I don't understand. Dave grunts. Dad tells the one about the farmer's daughter and the three Wise Men. Dave grunts again. Then he tells one about a farmer who gets very upset because he sees that the neighbor's son has pissed his name in the snow under his daughter's window.

"Now, Bill," says the neighbor. "There's no real harm in that. We both used to do that out in front of Betty Shaw's house. Don't you remember?"

"Yeah, yeah," says the angry farmer. "But this time the name was in *my daughter's handwriting*."

Dave grunts very loudly at this. Dad chuckles and starts another one. I listen hard for my godfather. He must be just on the side of the tent where I can't quite see him. I wonder what he's doing and why he doesn't say more. Then I hear my father . . . "'Now,' said the husband. 'If you want to have sex, just squeeze my penis once—and if you don't want to have sex, squeeze my penis forty-five times.'" Dad pauses, waiting for my godfather to laugh. Dad's back is still to me. I hear a grunt. It doesn't really sound like Dave. Come to think of it—it doesn't really sound human. I'm beginning to think Dave is off in the woods taking a crap. I hear another grunt. I wonder who my old man's talking to. We both hear another grunt and Dad starts wondering who in hell he's talking to, too. At last, he turns around. I wriggle forward, mouth open.

My father has for several minutes been washing up and telling off-color jokes to maybe not the largest—but unquestionably, indisputably and without a damn doubt—the *fattest* brown bear ever seen on the planet. Enormous. Rotund. Bloated. Obese. This is not a Jackie Gleason or John Goodman kind of plumpness. This isn't even a Fat

Albert or John Candy sort of bulk. No. This is more like the Haystack Calhoun of bears. Slabby, flabby—blubbery. Not a butterball bear, but an out-and-out blob. A slob. An obscenity.

"Jesus!" my father shouts. The bear grunts again, maybe hoping for another joke—and no doubt a half dozen fresh rainbow trout. The shovel and the toilet paper are gone so I realize now it's obvious where Dave is. Dad grasps this unfortunate truth at the exact same time and starts scrambling around beating on pots and pans like a maniac. It strikes me funny and for a moment I forget about the danger, even as frozen as I am with fear. Then my father starts grunting too. The bear is unimpressed. A terrible, hideous growling rips through the air and I suddenly smell the stench of the gut-bucket's breath. The hair stands up on my old man's head. I see him stoop down to pick up a trout that I figure he was saving for me. Then—just as he's about to chuck it at the bear, Dave appears on the edge of the pines.

He's heading toward camp at impressive speed—yelling like a lunatic, swinging the shovel around his head like a battle-axe—a berserker who's blown a gasket—a fisherman who's been forced to kick off his old army-surplus pants in the violated privacy of the sacred morning dump and now sees only blood. It's like Peter O' Toole in *Lawrence of Arabia*, charging the train. "No prisoners! No prisoners! You FAT-ASSED BEAR BASTARDDDDDDDDDDD!!!!!!!!!!"

Toilet paper flies. Dad is making a racket with the pans. The bear looks at Dad, and then at Dave and then—by God—he turns tail and wobbles into the woods in the other direction. Dave rushes up to the smoldering fire still swinging the shovel and shouting. Dad beats the pans like a tambourine. They're cranked up to a frenzy still and somehow they start—well . . .

They start to dance like savages, totally unaware of me. "We beat the Bear!" they chant. "We beat the Bear! Big Fat Bear!"

At last they break down laughing, gasping for breath. Dave says, "Were you scared?" and the old man answers "Does a bear shit in the woods?" and they start to laugh and dance again. Two grown men by a cold stream, wrapping toilet paper around their heads like turbans, clapping and stamping.

Such a small occasion in either of their lives—that crazy dance by the dying fire. But how immensely glad I was to be there—without them seeing me, without them really knowing. To catch a glimpse of them then, just for a moment, not as adults, or even as men—but as wild, foolish, golden, happy—invincible. Whatever it is we hope to be when we never grow up.

SOMETIMES YOU MUST
GET LOST MORE DEEPLY
TO LEARN THE SECRET
OF THE WAY OUT

THE GIFT OF EVIL

Age nine. We move, and for a while everything is fine. I get my first job, when Mr. Abernathy, who owns the One Hour Martinizing dry cleaner, spots me sitting on the floor in Lucky reading a Jughead comic book. He says, "How'd you like to earn some money so you could buy one of those things?"

It turns out he wants me to vacuum and sweep up the linoleum—clean the toilets. I like earning the money. I can buy my own Slurpees and Rick Brant books like *The Wailing Octopus* and *The Electronic Mind Reader.*

Then on an unusually hot day for spring, March 29, to be precise, as I walk home from school, my life changes forever—and I smell the blossoming rhododendron and hear the heavy buzzing of the butter-colored bees even now.

I could tell you that I was lured by a mentally disturbed boy twice my size and twice my age into a swath of dense bushes beside a then-abandoned and boarded-up Mother's Club and a long, straight fuse of cinder-smelling railroad tracks, which have since been torn out to make a kind of nature walk—to be anally raped and then very likely murdered—but I'm not sure you'd understand me.

What actually happened is that I stepped outside of time—I

walked right through a wall that is always there to be breached; we just don't know it under normal circumstances. Into the Other World.

I found myself in a sanctuary of Evil.

And I found myself.

Many, far too many are the times since, when I've gone back to that glade of rhododendron, with the bee-humming intimacy closing in around me.

The sweat smell of my attacker, alkaline and piercing. The lost-forever sense of the neighborhood, ordinary lives, the fuzz of daytime television drifting through the thick, still air. Just out of reach.

It changes you when you have to plead for your life as a fourth-grader. It changes you when you are overpowered by superior strength, you have your pants torn down and a thumb thrust up your anus, in preparation for a semi-erect rapist's penis—when you're told in slow, measured tones that what you see around you—the dense green shadows, the hypnotic blur of the bees—is the last thing you're ever going to see.

It changed me.

It brought forth an inner violence I didn't know I housed and carried—that I concealed. That inner Creature, sickened by the pleadings of the Other, the whimpering, the loss of hope and dignity, felt the jabbing pain of the first rectal violation—before the true, final assault and the squeezing, wringing of the promised hands on neck—and reached out.

The Creature grabbed a rock, a humble insignificant rock lying among the already dry grass, the shreds of Green Lantern comic books and teenage firecracker paper—and struck out with a fury I'd never known was inside. The rock said to the Creature, "This moment is not written in stone—there is still a door out, a door back, a door beyond. Believe in me and I will set you free."

I believed. But the Creature knew.

It came forth like a cornered animal, retaliating with a deftness and tactical precision I could never have achieved. In the face of greater bulk and power, the Creature knew what it had to do and reared up like the monster all embattled inhuman nature is. One hundred thousand years of to-the-death close-quarters conflict streaming through the nerve fibers like a river of pure black luminous fire.

Evil? We will show you evil, in a fistful of blood. Go back to the darkness you came from, for you have only summoned forth the Darkness you sought to reflect. Go back, Demon, before the manifestation of your skull is caved in and smeared like a crushed little butter-colored bee.

I emerged as if newly born from that glade of rhododendron, running without pants and bleeding down the tracks to a neighbor's house to call the police.

There's a certain sound blood makes when it's flicking from you as you flee, staining hot steel rails. It's a kind of quiet you can't stop hearing.

I'm still here—and I see that little boy without pants escaping from the rhododendron every day. Every day, he gets away to live on in me.

My ravaged schoolbooks were later found by my friends, torn up and scattered among the bushes and along the tracks. When I returned from a six-week spell with my grandmother, recovering from the incident, I understood it had been assumed that I'd been murdered—and so I was greeted as something of a local celebrity and legend, having come back from the dead.

And it was true. I had. But I couldn't have done so without the Creature.

That the Creature had, and has still, something mysteriously in common with the Demon has worried me every sweltering afternoon since. Yet I count that dark intimacy with a previously unknown side of myself as the price of continuance, the gift the Evil gave me.

Not so very long after, two other boys were sodomized and left as blue-faced rag dolls in live oak groves nearby. By the same individual? Some mysteries are not so easily solved.

Still, all these springtimes later, I believe I know exactly the words those two boys heard before they could no longer listen anymore. I think I know the sweet sharp scent of the armpit sweat they breathed—and the face the face made when the hands went out for them.

Brothers in death we might have been—but for the Creature.

Perhaps they noticed a distinct limp in the Demon from how I hurt him. But then again, maybe that only made him seem more vulnerable and believable. Maybe that was the ruse he ran with them, because he knew he couldn't catch them if they had a chance to run for their lives.

Maybe on that heat blur strip of California railroad track I didn't really get away, I just survived. I think about that on hot spring afternoons when the rhododendron is in bloom and the bees are droning—and my heart starts beating faster.

What does it mean to escape?

I think about that every day.

FIRE AND FORGET

I turned ten inside a giant tire, honoring the engineers and earth-moving machines of the Oroville Land Dam, and a memorial to a mummified Indian chief who disintegrated into dust the moment he was exposed.

The photograph is fuzzy because my father was embalmed with summer gin and there were hundreds of monarch butterflies snowing through the heat waves shimmering off the shale.

I'd just been retrieved from a kind of camp, where he hoped I'd recover from the incident involving the eighteen-year-old boy, the railroad bridge, and the rumor that I'd died.

I suspected that my dad wanted to take me away with him forever. What I didn't know was that he owed more money in Reno than he could get his hands on and that my mother was having an affair. What he was about to find out was that after two weeks of making ice cream and root beer, I still wasn't right in the head.

He made me pose with my arms and legs out like spokes. Then he squeezed the trigger. The shutter clicked and the cocoon turned like a wheel into dust, butterflies falling like photographs on fire.

I see the edges curl into wings, remembering the relief on my father's face when we crossed the Canadian border that summer. Maybe he believed we could escape that easily—he was like that.

I see myself creeping behind the kitchen at that camp where the teenage girls were washing dishes in their T-shirts and shorts, dancing to the Doors' "Light My Fire."

I wanted to smell the wet cotton clinging to their skin, but when they saw my face pressed to the cool mesh of the screen, I was so moved, I ran away.

I'd wander through school and drugs and women in a vicious circle of black rubber and squandered wings.

Even now there's no telling what I was fleeing from or toward. I was so eager and afraid to be found, I chose as my hiding place, the Wheel.

JUICE IN THE PAIL

One hundred miles from Thunder Bay we blew a gasket and overheated on a fresh-cut logging road, deep in the woods.

Dad was half-drunk and I was scared—of the silence, the distance, of the endless Ontario trees. Who did we expect to find back there? Whacko woodsmen drunk as ferrets, crawling with guns? You bet we did.

But the woods are weird precisely because they're unpredictable. We came across a chain saw resting against a pine. It was still warm. I remember the light between the trees, the empty quiet bigger than a single sound, all sadness, like a sudden change in moods.

Then the man who belonged to the chain saw appeared, hot wedges of gold spike-haloed around his head. He wore the plaid uniform of the tree-cutting man—arms huge from hefting the weapon of the woods.

One hand outstretched to us with a shiny pail full of blue bleeding berries fresh-picked by his calloused fingers.

We shared with this stranger the sweet juice of the northern berries, in the heart of his forest—half-shadow, half odd still light. We returned with him to the compound of trailers and shacks for Canadian bacon and blueberry flapjacks, then he towed us with one of the

Kenworths back to the main road—we could limp to town from there. But before he roared back down the dusty track, he gave us a plastic bucket of berries, still smiling at our surprise.

The town mechanic was surprised too—especially when he found out where we'd broken down. He pointed out that a campful of men alone in the woods can go a little loco sometimes. He claimed he'd found two hunting dogs beheaded by a small lake the previous autumn—and a husband and wife had disappeared not far away—the story made all the regional headlines.

"Strange things happen in the woods," he wheedled, with a malignant local smile.

But Dad—his tongue still purple from the berry juice—had regained his faith. "Strange things happen," he agreed.

MOONLIGHT RIDER

Out of the wreckage, out of the rape, out of the rhododendron, down the railroad tracks, I made a realization—I had an epiphany. The one thing I could've changed in that heat flicker afternoon was how I was moving. If I hadn't been walking, I wouldn't have ended up running, and bleeding. Every moment of darkness hinges on some weakness that's gone overlooked. Think about that. I guarantee you, it's true.

The terror of the attack and the mythology that grew up around me after I reappeared in school after a six-week absence allowed me to see something I'd only felt, not fully perceived. I was walking home from school because I didn't own a bike, and I didn't own a bike *because I didn't know how to ride one.* I'd never been taught. Swimming, fishing, skiing, horses—anything that my parents wanted to do—the opportunities were open. But on the level of basic kid survival skills in the world that I inhabited?

Other kids were riding Stingray bikes with banana seats. Not me.

My father got me driving, not just out in the desert, but in real metro traffic as a child. A child. Riding a bike? Nope. My sister had a bike, with a basket too, but I don't recall her ever riding it. It just sat in the garage collecting dust.

Why didn't we ever ride bikes as a family? Because it would've been too normal? I used to ride a tricycle around in the house, for God's sakes. We'd been blindfolded and shoved into water. Hooded on ponies. There's an old tinted photograph of my mother as a child on a smaller version of a penny-farthing in a Little Orphan Annie dress. Why did we miss this lesson? No answer.

One morning Dad moved out—and I started running everywhere.

But after the rhododendron, it dawned on me one afternoon. No one was going to help me solve the problem that I'd come to grasp. Only I could do that. So, I dusted off my sister's greasy girl's bike and pulled down our garage door. It was a big deal in those days for a boy to be seen riding a girl's bike—especially if he didn't know how to ride one at all.

It will sound somewhat pathetic to admit that I first tried learning inside our garage. It didn't occur to me at first that I was attempting to maneuver in a space that actually required maximum skill. After about the third collision with a wall, a few boxes knocked over, a scrape in an oil smear on the concrete, I began to see the situation. I needed space. Open space. I had to get up to some speed. I had to risk taking a tumble, but I needed to be somewhere where others couldn't see me fail. Training wheels? That would've only been more humiliation. I was way past that point. I could see only one possible solution.

The single nearby location where I was sure I wouldn't be observed—that was open enough and flat enough—was the school playground at night. I couldn't go to the shopping center parking lot—there would always be somebody passing by on the main road. No one would be at the school at night. I'd have all that black asphalt to skin myself on in private. But I'd have to walk my sister's goony girl's bike past the place where I'd seen my life nearly end, in the dark when everyone (hopefully) was sleeping. And I needed a full moon so I could see. A light on the bike wouldn't do. Not for a beginner, a virgin on two wheels. (I'd later come across a line in a book of Japanese poetry . . . *Be wary of all worlds in which you cannot give birth to yourself.*)

The full moon came but a few days later, and I knew it was do it now or not at all. There's something of a relief in those kinds of crises. Everything for a moment at least becomes clear and sharply outlined. Like the pine trees and ominous shapes of parked cars. I couldn't sleep after the attack anyway.

As soon as my mother and sister had fallen asleep (and without Dad in the house they were scared too), I'd climb up on the roof in a blanket, where I could see in all directions. It was cold, even at that time of year, come early morning. But it was safe. I could watch the shadows of the little men who lived in the juniper . . . and the earwig soldiers. The neighborhood was alive with things and beings wanting to get me. Still, I knew that the greatest danger lay waiting for me on my way to and from school. That's when I was really alone, except for the Creature, and he scared me almost as much as the Demon. Riding a bike would give me speed and another way to come home. Freedom. It wouldn't keep me from being ambushed again. It wouldn't keep the fear away . . . but it would help.

So, I took the longest walk of my life down that fallen ladder of iron moonlight with my sister's bike—fresh oil on the chain. Dogs barked in the distance. I saw a couple of cats prowling. All along the old Southern Pacific railroad line that spanned the valley was a jungle of cottonwoods, swamp oak and sumac . . . remnants of forts and hideouts kids had made of cardboard boxes. Things moved in the branches and in the mess of blackberries that had sprouted up over the drainage culvert. Rats maybe, raccoons, but not mad hoboes, not the Demon.

Arriving finally at the darkened school was at first a gigantic relief—and a mystery. The moon made sheets of diamonds of the classroom windows, all the desks waiting silently, filled with erasers and rulers, orange peels and wads of gum . . . the SRA Reading Laboratory boxes on the table beneath the chalkboard, with their color-coded cards (everything needed to have some hint of the laboratory in those days).

I thought of how I'd been huddling in the back of the library after school buried in *The Wonderful Flight to the Mushroom Planet* . . . *Rifles for Watie* . . . and *Homer Price* (I liked the story about his unstoppable doughnut-making machine).

It seemed very odd to hear the school so quiet—so still in fact I could hear the big clocks ticking in the classrooms even through the windows. Although I'd missed weeks, I could recount where every single member of my class sat, only they weren't there.

It had never occurred to me before to think about the secret life of empty classrooms . . . the dead flies the janitor Mr. Kosesky hadn't found . . . the maps . . . the boxes of pipe cleaners and Styrofoam balls. What went on when we weren't there. *They made us square dance on rainy days. I pledge allegiance to the flag . . . my book report is about . . .*

I found the darkness and the silence hypnotic. Then I remembered why I was there. It was time to face the challenge.

The moonlight made the monkey bars and the jungle gym look unearthly . . . things arrived from outer space. I was suddenly afraid. But I got on the bike.

I steered between the four-square blocks and the hopscotch boxes. I teetered. I wobbled. I fell over and banged my knee. But the moment I let the wheels roll I found I could make a turn. The bike wanted to go—it did the work—all I had to do was pedal and steer. The sheer, smooth field of the blacktop glazed with moon made me feel like I was sailing over water. I shot around the tanbark where the slide and the swings were. I circled! I flew! My legs pumped and pumped, and I learned after but one crash, how to use the brakes. I learned how to change gears between the three speeds. Even when I really wiped out because I'd taken a corner too sharp, sprawled on the hard surface, staring up at the sky seemed like discovering some local heaven. I saw a satellite.

For two hours I whizzed around and mastered the bike so completely I could do the forbidden thing of riding in the corridors, all vacant now, doors locked, only once bounding off the walls, but never losing control. I vowed I would ride everywhere after that. I didn't care if I was riding a girl's bike. I'd go back to my job at the dry cleaner's and make enough money to buy my own Schwinn three-speed. Bright green. Then I could ride to the Plaza shopping center where a man wearing a welder's mask had robbed the Wells Fargo Bank. I could ride to school. I rode all the way home.

The fear would come back. The Demon and the Creature, too, weren't to be left behind so easily, but still, I learned a great lesson that night. I taught myself. When some of the light inside you is stolen, risk a bit more darkness to steal some of the moonlight back. Whenever I've fallen, ever since, in any way . . . I think of those rusted spokes tick-turning silver in the moonshine out on that proving ground playground. I think of riding, almost flying, past the place where I nearly died, my own blood mingled with the rust on the rails.

I think of that night I walked out alone, heart thudding, through the shadows to meet the moon—and how I rode home with it in a basket. Never quite as alone again, yet not as haunted.

OFF RAMP

My stepbrother and I rode our bikes without lights down the steep hill that would whip you straight onto the freeway, heading for the bridge. The centrifugal speed was intense. The design of the on-ramp was so bad the view was basically blind. If a car was coming you were history. That was the beautiful simplicity of the challenge.

You had to whoosh the curve, push hard on the straightaway, glide across four lanes, then pump, drive, fly for the off-ramp a quarter mile down. The chute was sharp, steep and coiled like a spring. Grinding for speed across the freeway, you couldn't afford to brake until you were clear of the lanes. Then you had to worry if someone came up behind you fast because all you had was a tinny little reflector on the back—not to mention the very real possibility of crashing into the sides or losing control down at the bottom when you were well advised to shoot the too-abrupt traffic light and bogart for the darkness of a side street so the cops didn't burn you.

It was a marvelous thing to be hiding alone down at the very bottom, heart still thudding, between the streetlights on a misty night, listening for the ticking of a certain set of bicycle wheels, knowing that once more you'd made it, that you'd cheated that dark wild thing. Listening. Waiting for a shadow, very like your own, to emerge out of the fog.

CAPTAIN GALAXY COMES BACK TO EARTH

His real name was Ron Walsh, but I knew right away when my father introduced him that he was Captain Galaxy, the star of one of our local children's TV shows. Every afternoon for years, I'd watched and cheered when his spaceship took off. In the very early days, it was an old rocket ship with rivets and bolts, filmed in black-and-white. Over the years, he got a shiny chrome flying saucer and slipped slowly into color.

He wore a bright orange space suit and grinned and waved—and was given a sharp black baseball cap with a red comet emblem when he started losing his hair. He introduced shows like *The Whirlybirds* and cartoons like *Peter Potamus*. He invited kids in for quizzes and special prize drawings in the Control Room (how many kids wanted to have a Control Room?).

He was such a constant and larger-than-life part of my growing up, the thought of meeting him in the flesh had never occurred to me. How could I? He was off in his spaceship—or as I grew older—off in some studio made to look like a spaceship. He certainly wasn't out playing golf in the middle of the day with a nutty psychologist who drank with his alcoholic clients and a young boy on the verge of insanity.

But that's where I met him. At the Chabot Golf Course in the hills of Oakland, where years before, my father had baptized me in a water hazard. Dad was a very keen golfer. In fact, one of the great crises in his postwar, post-divorce, post-heart-attack life was when he was playing a round alone early one morning and he hit a hole in one—nobody there to see it. Boy, did that irk him. He had to write a sermon about it. He called it "Your Whole in One," and it was about whether good deeds or triumphs have to be witnessed by other people to be real—doesn't God see everything? My mother called it "The Sermon on the Green." Anyway, I was eleven years old and Dad would let me hit a few shots on every hole, and make believe I was his caddy. Ron was staring down a long green fairway speckled maddeningly white with thousands of little daisies, trying to locate his ball. "You know," he said, winking at me, "I have this dream. It's a recurring dream. I'm searching for a daisy in a field of golf balls."

He'd seen enough kids to know there was something not right with me. Sometimes the fear would overcome me in midsentence—an idiot blankness sucking all the oxygen out of the air. How could I explain it? How could I be clear in the bright sunlight surrounded by green grass and the cool menthol of the eucalyptus? I moved and breathed minute by minute. And that was fine by him. "You know what the pro over at Round Hill told me?" he asked. "Relax in the back swing. Just loosen your grip, let it happen. So I did—and you know what happened? I hit him with the three-iron."

His firm belief was that the key to a successful round of golf was a cheeseburger in the grill afterward, with a crisp, cold pickle and a basket of French fries. We sat there chomping away under a glossy poster of Jack Nicklaus blasting out of a sand trap (what could be sadder than grown men worshipping professional golfers?), and he told me how they filmed the spaceship—about gaffes with the kids in the audience, like the little boy who peed on the navigation console, or the girl with the glass eye that popped out and got crushed by a camera man. It didn't occur to me that mishaps and unforeseen circumstances were a fact of life for everyone. And on television? Wasn't everything rehearsed, even when it didn't seem like it?

Simple things like dumb jokes and a cheeseburger were more important than I'd realized. My world had collapsed inside itself so that almost no surprises could happen—or if they did, they only added to the fear. Everything seemed linked, planned, designed, aimed and geared toward frightening and humiliating me. When I was alone at home waiting for my mother and sister to return from wherever they were, I'd take refuge on the roof. From there I could defend and be on watch on all sides of the house. I learned that from Zorro. The importance of the high ground. I could, if worst came to worst—which of course it would—leap over the fence. There was no evil capable of catching me in either the walnut grove behind our house (which I knew well enough to run through at full speed on a moonless night and where I had many hiding places) or the Hatcher's backyard next door. The Demon couldn't get me.

But I thought of sad Mr. Wyman, who leapt to his end from a roof. And I thought of Neil Armstrong and Buzz Aldrin, leaping from their space capsule into the dust of the Sea of Tranquility.

Have you ever jumped off a roof? It takes careful, painful, paratrooper astronaut practice, especially to do it really well in the dark. In those dark days, I was on the roof almost every night. I'm not sure where my sister was then. She maintains she was home looking after me while our mother was out cavorting with various men—which I'm sure was true on many nights. But some nights she'd be out at friends' houses, and in winter, the darkness fell early. Men on the moon.

In any case, I got to where I could hurl myself off the edge, clear a six-foot wire fence eight feet from our house, tuck, roll and run—and if the Hatchers weren't home, scramble up onto their roof from on top of their garbage cans and be in position to leap for the shingles of Marilee Thomas's garage if need be. I could move like a cat. Not because I wanted to or because it came naturally to me. No one was ever more afraid of climbing a tree. I became a suburban astronaut and an artist of evasion in spite of my instincts. I developed new instincts, and there's nothing more exhilarating or terrifying than that.

Each night, I became quieter, stealthier, slipping out from first my room, then when the fear grew too great, my sister's bedroom—sometimes even my mother's bed. There was the Demon to worry about—the earwig soldiers and the juniper men. And always the half-seen things in the streetlit darkness—luminous—all gill, claw and feeler. I grew keener and quieter.

But the price paid was an increasing invisibility, a fading. I knew that one day I would be fear itself. One night I'd be able to see in the dark because I was darkness. I'd fly because I couldn't fall. I'd have crossed over into that realm that lay beyond the walnut grove. I knew in my thumping heart that the familiar neighborhood nights of automatic sprinklers and Manchurian pear trees masked a shadowland of breath and scent, undead faces, unknown threats and predators waiting like trap-door spiders. Suddenly, I felt the green of the golf grass and the pink of Jack Nicklaus's shirt signaling to me, calling me back.

Captain Galaxy was suspiciously good company for me that day, and I wondered if my father might've had an idea in mind—and perhaps more than an idea, a true therapeutic technique, for which I'd never given him credit. He was, as I came to see, an unorthodox thinker that way. It was another one of those days that helped change my life.

Although I didn't realize it at the time, you don't lose your mind all at once. And you don't find the way back all at once. It's a gradual process that can often look in the moment like getting more lost. I thought of these things. About the grace of everydayness. About what and whom I really feared. About my father and his peculiar brand of healing, which in the end did him so much harm.

But what I thought about most of all was what my father said when he drove me home. I asked what was wrong with Captain Galaxy. Dad looked at me for a moment as if he was going to stop the car—I think because it struck him that everyone I saw him with was one of his counselees. Then he turned to me and said, "It's not about being wrong; it's about feeling better. If you think there's something wrong with people, than you want them to be right. I want people to feel better."

"Does Captain Galaxy want to feel better?" I asked.

"Yes, he does. He just has great mood swings that he can't control. Sometimes he's all revved up, or relaxed and funny—other times he feels so bad he can barely get out of bed. At his worst, he feels suicidal. He wants to die."

I was very sorry about that. The thought of his shiny spaceship crashing struck me as a great tragedy.

Many things happened in the weeks and months that followed. I started sleeping in my own room again (a big step) and actually in my bed instead of under it, or sneaking out to huddle on the roof. I finally went back to school. My mysterious and long absence had made me something of a legend. I had to take several tests to prove I shouldn't be held back a grade. I passed pretty easily, thankfully. The thought of being kept back was hellish.

I was picked for teams again and even captained some. I was confided in. Once a boy named Terry Williams ridiculed me and I threw him against a pole in the hallway and he slumped to the concrete. Gradually my grades returned to normal. I even stepped ahead.

Meanwhile, my father remarried. He had a new family and so did I, including a stepbrother my age. The days went by and the old fears seemed to fade. I could look out my window at night and not see the shadowland. The metallic perspiration scent of the Evil became rarer.

My father moved out of his apartment in Berkeley to a drafty house in Oakland, just off College Avenue. I saw him and the new family almost every weekend—every other one at least. Captain Galaxy lived only a few blocks away, although we didn't call him that anymore. The show had sadly been canceled, after all those years. But I think part of him was glad about it.

Because he'd been a childhood hero, I'd never considered that his role was something of an embarrassment to him. Often we saw him for parties and he got Dad tickets for things. He had a lot of connections around town, but you could tell by the way people talked about him that he was a source of amusement. Everyone seemed to know his catch cry . . . "Now, Star Team Troopers, it's time for . . . " I think it got on his nerves. He'd become an executive at the station and did some community theater (he even had a bit part in a Clint Eastwood *Dirty Harry* movie). But he didn't look happy. He set up a bay fishing weekend for Dad, me and my stepbrother, but he got so smashed and seasick we never saw him on deck.

Ron, as we came to call him, had long before been through the divorce shredder, only his ex-wife had moved to San Diego and he rarely saw his kids. Then his second marriage broke up. After that he had a fling with an eighteen-year-old, which raised some eyebrows—not an easy thing to do in the Bay Area, and in those days almost impossible. I didn't know what to think of his third wife, and from the looks of things, neither did Ron. To be honest, I didn't really care much about him at that point, even though we'd come to know him as a neighbor and family friend. I associated him with the dark time—or with the lost time that came before—and I was too caught up in my own recovery, the changes in my body at the onset of puberty, a growing attraction to girls, whether it was Debbie Blee or Miss January. I'd come back from the shadows of the dead, having leapt off the roof for the last time. Almost the last time.

I found that my training regimen had made me far more agile and daring than I'd expected, which was a good thing, as my stepbrother was already a mass of scars and colorful stories. Together, he and his friends—Carlos (who might've become the first famous Hispanic magician had he not died in a car accident), Petey, a big pasty-faced Danish boy with a bowl haircut, and Fergus, a little black cigarette thief who was later blinded by an M-80—developed a gung-ho version of hide-and-seek called Lights Out. It was free-form and allowed for the creation of conspiracies and alliances. The one basic idea was to scare the shit out of people.

The game, as the name suggests, was best played at dusk going into dark and made use of the most extreme hiding places, such as neighborhood roofs, the underbellies of cars—wherever it was most challenging. (Each of the core players had his own unique style, so that you could just glance down a street and know right away how Carlos had seen it . . . the options he might've considered . . . and that became a critical part of the art . . . to both follow your signature style yet to keep surprising everyone, outdoing your last masterpiece.)

We eventually had between twenty and thirty kids participating at any one time. Every time we went hunting for each other, in daylight or darkness, some adventure took place, some vision. Balanced on a section of rusted rain gutter, about to fall fifteen feet into a rose arbor, I watched Mrs. Broadbent kneel by her bed to pray, then take out her teeth and kiss them. Once, my stepbrother ran a whole block on the hoods of cars to get away from a savage Doberman and even then had to beat it off with the bicycle chain he wore as a belt.

Smushed snails on the sidewalk. Held breath, pounding hearts. The adrenalin and innocent danger was immensely therapeutic for me. We literally worked our bodies into the palings and the vines of the neighborhood. There were sprained ankles, broken fingers, bruised knuckles and scabbed elbows. We were lucky it wasn't a lot worse. Some kids we didn't even know except by nickname—like Drumstick or Gooey—joined in. No one ever telephoned or made an appointment. No one was texting on a cell phone then. We'd all come in on a different kind of beam and find each other without knowing how.

My father and my new stepmother were generally silent regarding our activities (my mother said they let us run wild). I think my father reasoned that too close a questioning would only bring to mind the famous Christmas Eve, when in full Santa Claus regalia (complete with sleigh bells), he got stuck out on the very steep roof of our house in Berkeley (following a few too many eggnogs) and had to be rescued by the fire department. It had happened many years before, when my father was convinced I needed to believe in Santa a while longer. I think my sister was in on it. I appreciated the effort—and the risk of breaking his neck. Having come to understand quite a bit about roofs, I grasped just how much gumption (or eggnog) it would've taken. Still, the slightest hint of that night in the past could set me laughing again, the sight of the old man clinging to the chimney for dear life, cold stars overhead. Best to let us go our hidden, hunting ways, he figured. Besides, he was smart enough to know that anything he was even vaguely aware of that we were up to was but the tip of an iceberg. (How true that was.)

Lights Out would've gone on a lot longer had it not been for his birthday.

It happened over an unusually warm Easter. A big barbecue on the new redwood deck out back. Lots of Dad's old cronies and clients showed up, including Ron Walsh and his newish wife Phyllis, who looked very uncomfortable, perhaps because Ron insisted on bringing a bottle of Seagram's, with a look in his eyes like he'd been into another one before they arrived.

My stepbrother and I were allowed a can of Coors each, which at age twelve seemed like a big deal in public. We savored the brew slowly. But all the adult talk of Freud and fondue bored us, so after the burgers were devoured, we felt the forces reaching out. The tribe was gathering. Time to play our stalking game. So we headed off. But Ron Walsh wanted to come too. We didn't know what to say.

"Why don't you take it easy?" Dad asked, with uncharacteristic restraint. "Here," he said, handing over some corn on the cob wrapped in tin foil.

"Negative, Lieutenant," Ron said. "The Captain must lead his people."

"I think they'll be all right on their own," Dad remarked, as pointedly as I ever heard him say anything. Several people made comments, but Ron wasn't to be dissuaded.

"C'mon honey," Phyllis chided. "You'll make a fool of yourself."

"That's never worried you before."

It was very awkward. He was swaying, trying to get a cigarette lit. I opened my mouth to say something, but he waved me down.

"What's the matter Star Steam Stroopers, don't you think the Captain can hack it? A little hide 'n' seek? Christ, I've been doing that my whole life. You just watch old Uncle Ron. He will disappear before your eyes. He *is* a professional entertainer, don't forget. A thesss-pian."

We didn't want to be cold, and we could see the way the other adults were turning on him. So, my stepbrother quietly explained the way Lights Out worked—the ambush rules, the tactics. This was no pissy olly-olly-oxen-free party game that would be over in a few minutes. It was serious business. It could take hours and cover several blocks—and my stepbrother was going to be It.

Ron nodded to all these instructions and warnings. He seemed to sober up. At least some of the grown-up weariness and cynicism seemed to leave him. Then we were off, fifteen or so of us scattered into the streets where cats hissed at us and oil pans dripped. I hoped Ron would be found quickly and go home.

We strayed over fences and through cypress borders, each of us breaking off on our plan. The late afternoon light began to fade. Carlos snaked out his hands from under an old mattress and grabbed a kid called Weird Willy by the ankles. Willy got so spooked he bit off the end of his tongue. Petey and Drumstick formed an alliance with Krazy Katie, a light-skinned black girl, who carried a Filipino flick knife with a tiny flashlight built in, and together they chased the twins all the way to the chain-link fence of the abandoned car wash and pelted them with tanbark before pulling their pants down.

My stepbro was in fine form, staring through walls and around corners. He nailed five people in the first hour, which meant he had a formidable team to hunt with. But they didn't find me. At one point, three of them were prowling around a front yard on Florio, where an old woody station wagon was parked, with a canoe on the roof. I was inched up under the canoe, thinking I could get all three of them, which would make them mine—but I wasn't sure I could scare them sufficiently from such an awkward position—and then the people who lived in the house peeked out the window and everyone ran off. I was the one who got a big scare then, because this red-haired guy came out and headed for the woody. I only just escaped. He yelled something as I bolted.

Sprinting openly down the street was the most dangerous thing you could do. That's when you were totally vulnerable. I made for a little garden shed that I'd used before. It was kept locked, but there were two boards in the back that were loose, so you could crawl through. There was a rat's nest in there, and it smelled of snail pellets and fish emulsion, but I didn't care.

When I got alongside I heard something that made me stop. At first, I had this funny idea that Ron Walsh was in there. I listened closely. Definitely breathing—but then a sticky, squishy noise. I crept down on all fours and stuck my eye up to a slit. There was just enough light to make out Donny Chandler. He was sitting down, leaned up against the door, with his dick out of his pants. It was hard. Every once in a while he'd spit on his hand and stroke the shaft.

A thrill came over me. I wasn't sure exactly what I was seeing—only that I wasn't supposed to. Danny was older, our family didn't talk about sex, and because of the rape, I was shy about all that stuff. But I knew not only could I scare him to death, I'd have him in a real corner. He'd be so embarrassed he'd do anything for me not to tell. It made me almost laugh out loud. I was so eager to bust in on him I could barely contain myself. He was dead meat.

But I liked watching him. Not because I wanted to see his dick, although there was something nasty and real about it that was intriguing. I liked the power I had over him then. For those few moments, listening to him—spying on him in that old garden shed that smelled of rat piss and fish guts—I held his neighborhood reputation in my hands. Carlos and Krazy Katie would've eaten him alive if they'd known. But I couldn't bring myself to. It didn't seem right. I ran away and went to hide in a Salvation Army bin, trying to gather my thoughts. I actually fell asleep in there, and woke up stiff and cramped.

I took the longest way home I knew, and by the time I got there, it had been dark for some time. My stepbrother was in the front yard waiting to hit me with a lemon. He never missed. He said no one had found Ron. In all the commotion about the canoe and Donny whacking off, I'd forgotten about Captain Galaxy. Maybe he was better at hiding than we thought. Or maybe he'd just gotten bored—or thirsty. We went inside and snacked on leftovers.

At nine o'clock, Ron's wife rang and said that he wasn't home. Dad was a little worse for wear from the party, but he got us to join him on a walk through the neighborhood. We felt sort of silly calling out, "Ron! Ron!" But the neighbors were used to odd stuff from us. No answer. No sign. When we got back, I could see Dad was worried. I figured Ron had just slunk off to a bar somewhere. Or maybe he was passed out. He'd come around when the temperature dropped.

Next morning, however, when Ron still hadn't shown up, any trace of anger or humor gave way to anxiety. Phyllis had even spoken to the police. Dad did another search of the neighborhood, which turned up nothing. I got to thinking about what Ron had said before we started playing—about how he was going to disappear before our eyes. It made me think of Dr. Madden, an orthodontist and gambler Dad had been counseling, who supposedly died down in Mexico. Only when the body came back in one of those silver airplane coffins—temporary coffins, they call them—it wasn't the right guy. Dr. Madden was never heard from again, and more than a few people thought he'd planned it that way.

The next day the cops were taking the matter seriously. Phyllis was beside herself. Three days later a man named Bledsoe, who lived a block over, noticed a smell. Mr. Bledsoe's house was one of the older ones around. Down the narrow space between his house and his neighbor's was an old boxed shed built into the wall. The box was clapboard to harmonize with the house, with a heavy shingled lid on rusted hinges. The lid was hard enough to raise when outside, standing on firm ground. From inside, it would've been far more difficult. A young boy couldn't have done it.

But what Ron couldn't have known, until it was too late, was that the box was connected to an old coal chute that had once run down to the furnace in the basement. As the coal furnace had long ago been replaced by an oil burning one, the coal chute had been blocked off. Unfortunately, the chute had been sealed up from the basement side. In climbing into what he probably thought was an old storage box for wood, Ron fell down far enough into the chute to get himself wedged. Drunk, confused, he might've struggled. Bledsoe hadn't been home at the time, and none of the other neighbors heard. The medical opinion, which my father conveyed to us as sensitively as he could, was that the cause of death was a heart attack.

Phyllis Walsh never blamed us openly for what happened, and she was as polite and controlled as could be at the memorial service, for which Dad put on his ministerial robes for the first time in several years. But she never spoke or waved to us again in the street. A few months later she moved to San Francisco. The details of the death were respectfully kept out of the media. My father gave the eulogy and some of Ron's colleagues from the TV station spoke about his contribution to broadcasting and the community, which were confirmed by many tributes.

I'd never stop thinking of Captain Galaxy after the moment we found him, curled like a fetus, his face discolored—a mix of terror and resigned peace. How kind he was to me that first day on the golf course. How black it must've been inside that box at the end. In dreams sometimes, I go back to that box and open the lid—but I don't find a dead man or a boy inside. I see a bright green fairway full of daisies. At the far end, way off in the distance, I see myself, poised on my mother's roof as the sun goes down. I remember what it was like to be scared—so scared I couldn't even say what it was that I was afraid of anymore. I remember what it was like to leap into the dark. How good it felt when I finally fell home.

THE FLAMINGO CONSPIRACY

If you'd been going to classes with the same kids, boys and girls together the whole time—what would you think if one morning Mrs. Kremser ushered all the girls out of the multipurpose room and Mr. Wallace ordered all the boys into the gym?

Would it worry you if your routine of building California missions out of sugar cubes and inflating flabby wet chunks of cow lungs with Sweetheart straws was suddenly interrupted by a forty-five-minute film on *waterbirds*?

We weren't stupid; we knew something was up. But we were trapped, forced to learn about cormorants, penguins, petrels, puffins, ibises and heron—all of us dead curious, of course, about what was going on with the girls. We even missed them a little.

Grant Dorset, who was two years older than the rest of us, thought he knew what was happening, so naturally Carl Spock claimed he knew too, but I didn't trust either of them because they once put out a cigarette in my ear.

It was hard to pay attention to the birds, being so curious and all, but the colors were very bright and the sound was turned way up, so I actually started to get interested, especially in the flamingos—then suddenly the reel ended and everybody was knocking over chairs to get out to the blacktop, where all the girls were milling around, smiling strangely.

"You don't think they saw a film on landbirds?" asked Dieter, the butterball with the bristly hair we gave knuckle burns to.

"Jesus, Dieter! Act your age, not your IQ," said Noel, as he ran over to quiz the girls. Like us, he figured as soon as we got a hold of the Blabbermouth, Nancy Strange, we'd get to the bottom of the mystery, but even she was very coy.

It felt like something mysterious had happened. The girls were acting like they'd been let in on a big secret, as if they'd somehow gotten older than us in only an hour.

Then Noel came running back with his report. "They saw a movie too," he said. "It was about a red dress."

"A red dress?" we all said.

"Yeah, this little girl grows up into a real girl and her mother buys her a red dress. The rest was all about washing up. You know, about keeping clean and stuff."

"Jesus! Who'd want a red dress?" said Paul Marhenky.

"What's the matter, Stinky, do you wanna blue one?" said Noel as he ran off to climb the backstop, thinking the puzzle solved.

I wasn't satisfied, though, so after social studies I cornered Lonnie Child, who kind of liked me, and she told me the movie was about bleeding and how babies are made. She told me that girls have eggs inside them, but not like the kind of eggs you buy at Safeway. Then she told me that boys have this kind of milk inside them—full of little swimming things with tails like tadpoles. It was enough to make you sick.

She said girls get eggs and bleed. Boys get directions, then the boy sticks his wiener in the girl's angina and squirts tadpoles that mix with her eggs and one of the eggs becomes a baby unless the boy wears a balloon.

I didn't know what to say to that. I tried to tell her that we learned about eggs too. I told her about the flamingos, but she didn't care. She said we got the wrong film. We were supposed to see one about wieners and tadpoles, but someone got confused and we got flamingos instead. I figured she was confused, or the teachers had told her to say all that—that it was part of the big trick being played on the boys.

Things just weren't the same anymore. I watched Amy Swanson stomp out of a perfectly good dodgeball game because she claimed it was "immature." The way she strutted past a group of boys who were fighting by the drinking fountain reminded me of one of the birds in the movie. Then I looked at Lonnie and her cheeks flushed *bright pink*. She was playing with her hair, *shifting from one leg to the other*. I wanted to talk to some older kids—to find out if anything weird had happened to them. What else weren't we told? First my father claimed I came from God, then Mr. Gaskell, our science teacher, tells us we're really made of pieces of dead stars. Now Lonnie was telling me I was full of tadpoles and that I'd once been an egg, and had only been born because my father didn't wear a balloon when he got directions. It was pretty clear to me. Somebody was lying.

Noel thought so too, so after school we took his Daisy gun down to the dump and shot up Dr Pepper cans and tried to work it all out. We gave the matter some serious thought and what Noel came up with made me feel better. He said, "I don't know about the flamingos and stars, but Dieter's a tadpole if I ever saw one, and if I were you, I'd still ask Lonnie to the carnival. It's not her fault she's got eggs."

So I asked her, and she said yes, and I bought her black licorice ropes and a strawberry snow cone and she got sick on the Scrambler, and two weeks later the tadpole film came just like she said it would, and while we laughed at the pictures of penises, the girls had to watch a movie about the building of the Hoover Dam, and Noel tricked Dieter into sitting in rubber cement . . . and I was right about things never being the same again.

REINDEER GAMES

Don't ask me why it was important—it just was. Christmas had become all about blowing up fake fat snowmen and stealing reindeer from the roof of the Rexall drugstore.

It was Layne who led us. We used to laugh at him and call him names, until he beat us senseless or did things we never dared to do.

On top of the drugstore, we looked for the Star of Bethlehem but found only the guard lights of the lumberyard and the faint glow of the front room, where my German shepherd had scratched the chrome table before the vet put her to sleep.

Then Layne wrenched Rudolph out by the roots and slit the anchor rope with a Tijuana switchblade and we began the difficult descent.

"Don't worry so much, you sissies," he said. *If you get stuck, just jump. It's like climbing, only backwards.*

Who knows how the cop car came to be waiting by the Dumpster below—it was one of those bad-luck breaks. But we knew we were done for, all of us reconciled to capture—except for Layne. He was the one carrying Rudolph and we all bet he'd be the one quickest to bolt when we hit the ground.

But he had invited us on a mission that night, and he refused to abandon his prize or us. So he battered a bewildered cop with a plastic reindeer while his buddies scattered down the tracks, where the cop car couldn't go. Then, even then, rather than fling the stupid thing away, Layne ran with Rudolph crumpling and cracking underneath his arm, because it was just a silhouette. Damn him if he didn't beat us to the trestle, where we laughed, knowing we were safe.

* * *

Four years after the robbery of the reindeer, Layne followed Jorge Pacheco off the school bus for a fight behind the Chevron station. One minute they were standing in the sunlight, relaxing for combat . . . the next minute . . . Jorge was lying beside an oil drum bleeding badly from the head and twitching—and Layne was running down the tracks again. Those same tracks I'd run down.

I can see him sprinting through the black and golden bars of late May shade—then suddenly he turns to look at me and *the stars are bright behind him, the shadow of antlers blooming out of his head*—like something wild that's crept unwittingly into town—cornered in the long railroad moonlight.

And in that same eye or heart or hope, they never catch him for killing Jorge, who died in the ambulance. They never teach him to lick a toilet clean or to suck a cock at knifepoint. He doesn't fade into youth custody, to escape and get sent to real jail, never to escape the system ever again. On the bridge of his last midnight, he chooses a refuge where no cop car or convict can pursue.

So, he's not pacing out with lowered eyes a lime green cell somewhere—he's still laughing all the way down the long ladder to the light, which is just like darkness, only backwards.

HAREM SCAREM

Pubic hair was taboo, so I had mermaids in nylon, silk and suds glued to the walls of my tree fort—ladies who were later evacuated under emergency conditions to the floor beneath my bed.

Some will say that they instilled a false ideal of female beauty, or that they inspired at an impressionable age, the regrettable practice of collecting women like baseball cards. This may be true. But I would like to set the record straight on one very important point—*I never drew eyes on their nipples.*

The care I took with them embodied the fascination and respect we're quick to call love when the situation seems proper. So, when even my hiding place beneath the bed was raided, I stowed the loveliest survivors in sheaths of protective plastic in the vacant lot behind our house.

I thought I was saving them from a horrible fate, until I made the mistake of remembering to dig them up. Then I remembered the willow trees I'd seen in graveyards. The long cool branches dangling down to stroke the stones and the names, and the wreaths in the grass my father said was flesh.

WE LIVE FOREVER

My thirteenth birthday. I lose my baby fat. As the sun was coming up I'd pound down the silent streets. The cool, challenging smell of the morning—past Sandy Sweeney's house, which would be all dark and still. I was running after a black and red and white jersey, which the A team wore. I'd just missed the A team the year before and I wasn't going to miss it again. I was going to make the A team and then I was going to run right on into high school. I figured if I just started back far enough and got up enough speed . . . So, come 6 AM in any weather, I was running. Then I'd jump rope, grunt through sit-ups, and finally grab the barbell I'd bought by selling subscriptions to *Sunset* magazine and *Guideposts*, and I'd burn my muscles like bullfrogs soaked with kerosene. The position I wanted to play was halfback, which meant I'd have to knock off the best athlete in school—Miller King.

Three years earlier, I'd called him King Kong, and his gang chased me through the walnut orchards and caught me right at the gate to our house. I was almost in our backyard, safe, but they cornered me and I broke down crying. I would've given anything not to cry in front of them—in front of him—but I lost control of myself. Later, I watched Miller have a fight with Josh Donohoe's older brother in that same orchard. I was hiding behind a cool dusty-smelling walnut tree, feeling the texture of the trunk, and I made a promise to myself that I was going to remember *everything.*

A couple of weeks later, Miller King gave Daryl Steele, who was three years older, a bloody nose and a broken rib. He was going steady with Eve Warner, the girl with the biggest tits in the whole grade. He was already drinking beer and riding his older brother's motorcycle through the orchards late at night. I could never really like Miller after the day I cried in front of him, but I could never really hate him either.

Then one day in late August he took his younger brother out for a ride on the Suzuki and woke up in a world changed utterly. The brother had been catapulted off the back and had smashed into a tree. Permanently brain damaged. Miller, the school's best athlete, best fighter, regained consciousness to find he'd lost his right arm. The news stunned the school. In his suburban bedroom suspended in that lost orchard, one by one we came to pay our respects—to see the boy who fell from the sun—not a friend, but a fallen hero—wounded—vulnerable—as we'd never seen him before. Frightened—wan—naked—determined—boyish again in his deeper room. I realized I'd never been inside the King house before, even though I lived only five doors down and had seen Miller every day. His real father had died when he was a kid. His stepfather was an atomic scientist.

I'd never been close to him. The size and color of his room—the posters on his walls—were as unknown as the moons of Jupiter. And now to be there with others, peering in the doorway, pale sunlight leaking through the blinds and a vague hospital scent lingering like the clove and ammonia smell of uncertainty—we might all have been dead and risen to the ceiling of rooms we'd known and slept in and were now seeing for the first time—looking down at the body we'd been separated from.

He lay on the bed moving gently as if there were tiny needles underneath him. He was quiet and pale. He tried to smile. He did better than I would've, but I had the sad feeling that as much as he was glad to see us, our presence only worsened the impact of the misery and made the nightmare all the more real. In his stricken eyes I saw my father later lying in a hospital bed with a fat, dying heart, the tearful or grimly resigned faces of hospital waiting rooms, emergency rooms, hospices and the scenes of accidents. His fragile, unbelieving, yet still calm, powerful eyes were windows to all those moments of wreckage and agony.

I felt a tenderness for him I'd never known. He was many things I hated, but he was also for me that bigger something we all in some way aspire to be. It was a challenge to all I held sacred to see him fighting to smile back.

Every afternoon, with one sleeve pinned, he'd peer through the chain-link fence on the edge of the practice field, watching our scrimmages, searching for my number. I outdid his records in every category. The first time I touched the ball, in my black and red and white jersey, number 19, I scored a touchdown. I was sprinting down the sidelines with the crowd noise sweeping past and I noticed through the wind-stung corner of my eye, Eve Warner shaking her pompoms—for me. For me!

Yet somehow, what I was chasing eluded me. I gained eight hundred yards, scored fourteen touchdowns, caught twenty-two passes and threw a last-second game-winning TD pass myself from a halfback option. But I never went steady with Eve Warner. I never went steady at all. For two glorious days I held Shari Tomlinson's hand. I didn't know if I was supposed to do more. I was too shy to ask. And when I wasn't shy, I was petrified. And always when I turned, I seemed to see Miller watching me.

In dreams I go back to that neighborhood, not the real neighborhood you can walk around today, however changed, but that secret neighborhood we entered unbeknownst to our parents, the place of truth and danger—of terrible hopes and sorrow growing like ivy over fences crumbling away into the soft-smelling nights, where whispers linger in the air for years.

The bus that took us to junior high stopped in front of Miller's house and in that secret sense still does. Even the kids who are dead now, for surely some must've died since, are still there—the glow of our bodies moving in and out of shadow, the voices—funny, shy, cruel, challenging. Everything is still there in that perfectly broken orchard of light. There are G.I. Joe action soldiers and Barbie dolls buried in the dirt, a once-bright Tonka truck rusting under a juniper.

I'm coming down the street from my house and I know the name of the clouds I see because we learned the types in school. Cirrus clouds this morning, maybe cumulus later, or nimbus, or better still, a mackerel sky, those gentle ribbed undulations—and always a warm jasmine and ozone scent, like sex before we understood the smell.

There are girls laughing and playing with their hair, breasts beginning to form like time-lapse flowers opening in that Disney film we saw for science, *The Living Desert*. The girls aren't thinking of penises; they're thinking of shoulders and muscles, black eyes and bloody noses they've seen in playground fights and the spectacles behind rows of pine trees or down in the cardboard box wasteland under the bridge. Mr. Brose, who's running late to his boilermaker management job, rounds the corner in a Buick Riviera and seems to gesture at us, but what he's really doing is evaporating, like all our moments of wonder and chagrin . . . toys and dreams. The world trembles as Simon Bar Sinister threatens to make one of the stoplights stay red forever so the Macy's Thanksgiving Parade can't advance—and the late car quietly vanishes with Mr. Brose inside—just as the bus and time and the relentless crush of money and routine will take our bodies and our youth from us, leaving only the soft electric faces we wore when no one was looking . . . the smell of ozone mixed with Welch's grape jelly.

I see Miller. I see him as he was, tall, solid, somehow older than the rest of us.

I have a peanut-butter-and-jelly sandwich in a plastic bag advertised by the Man from Glad, and a Mickey berry pie or a pack of Hostess chocolate cream-filled cupcakes. The idea is to peel all the icing off and then suck the white foam from inside the sponge cakes. Josh Donohoe's black spiky hair and big white horse teeth bore me with talk about minibikes, David Mauren is overweight and constantly tells jokes about farts. Sad tough-guy Jeff Crowe really is handsome, I realize now, but he's got some kind of reading problem and has trouble with his temper—there's something hopeless about him even though he was good at kickball when we were younger. He reminds me of Carole Michelson, a tall afghan of a girl who goes from shy, stringy blonde with glasses to trippy drug babe who puts out for her older boyfriends. She keeps getting murdered even though we tell her not to hitchhike alone. Sometimes they find her body lightly covered with leaves by the side of the highway. Sometimes they have to use dental records to identify her because she's been missing for months and the body, when a famous psychic finally finds it, is badly decomposed.

Before she started fucking and drinking and knowing things, Carole would sometimes appear at the bus stop with a notebook pressed against her flat chest and sway so willowy and shy I felt sorry for her. But even as she twisted around all gawky and goofy, you could see the girl burning away to reveal a woman. It was terrifying in those days, to be at the mercy of such werewolf vampire changes. You never knew what would happen over summer. Chubby boys got tall and strong, scrawny girls got soft and full. But some of the most mysterious things, you couldn't see. There were foggy mornings sometimes, when the kids would emerge from the orchards of mist like zombies lumbering out of a black-and-white movie, *like the dead rising up out of the ground in the damp, potato-smelling air.*

But in the dream of Miller, the one-armed boy, there's no weather to speak of at first—then it seems to shift from glaring midday nothingness to a soft rose sunset, a little cold, like early October—the crunching brown leaf-bone and smoke scent will soon fill the air.

I have a confession to make to him. When his arm was torn off in the motorcycle accident, I found the bloody limb and took it home. I washed it and kept it hidden in an aquarium full of alcohol underneath my bed. I was afraid that if they found it, if they could sew it back on, then he'd be a football star again. For years I kept the arm secret, watching it float like some intermediate life form, afraid it would wriggle from the tank at night and come to strangle me. Finally, I had to bury the wrinkled, bloated and rotting thing in the orchard to free my mind. I've come back now to tell him, to ask his forgiveness, to go into the orchards, if any of them still remain, and dig the arm up. He has a bone to pick with me. Oh, yes. We must dig and find it among the walnut trees.

I'm walking up from the shopping center, where I vacuumed the dry cleaner's and where we climbed on top of the Rexall drugstore—where Mom gets her hair done, sitting under the time-machine, brain transplant bubble of the drier, knitting mechanically.

There's an old white wagon wheel out in front of Scott Dale's house, a row of stunted Monterey cypress trees that separate the house from the railroad tracks, or where they used to be. I approach the corner where the school bus is forever arriving and I see Miller as he was the last time, long ago, wearing a T-shirt under a down vest, the mutilated arm like something he's carrying, not a part of him. I'm watching him the way he watched me through the chain-link fence all those long practice afternoons ago and all those endless adult afternoons of making money ever since. The boy with a mangled shadow, laid out on the green blades with such ferocious tenderness; it grows larger and longer than any shadow possibly can. The boy with the invisible arm is full of black grass. He looks torn sometimes—when the sunlight blasts him against the rusted diamonds of the fence—like a doll that got chewed by a dog. Like Gus Gus. We live forever with those faces we begin with—the names we play and the games we can't forget.

I see you, Miller. Maybe the motorcycle accident that ended the life you'd known kept you young—and so I expect to find you still at home with the music pouring out of your suburban bedroom with the dirty underwear behind the door and *Penthouse* magazines stacked beneath the bed.

We live forever with those faces we begin with—the names we play and the games we can't forget—warnings and mysteries from the hidden world.

I see you still, Miller. And so I expect to hear Jimmy Page's guitar on *Houses of the Holy* drifting out your window into the orchard—where I once hid behind a walnut tree and watched you fight with both strong arms—and promised myself and time that I was going to remember . . . *everything.*

LOWERING HIM INTO THE TANK

It took four of them in sterile gowns with masks and latex gloves to hoist my father onto the hammock.

The motorized winch loosened the tiny links of chain and he descended into the stainless steel tank.

His fat face cringed. Not since the war hospital had he felt so raw—not until this daft laundry of nerves immersed him in the Hubbard tank.

His belly was, for the moment, unspeakable—gruesomely quilted with pig skin stretched over screen. His red legs grew flaccid. His gin-mill humor turned to quacks in the steam. But the stapled grafts of flesh kept seeping true, like spiderwebs fallen on a pond.

Each white, medical morning, they lowered him into a body of water, a clear young body with eyes that stared at us, at me.

"I think the water is deeper than it looks," I wanted to say.

But his blue eyes seemed to answer back—*water, like blood, is always deeper than it looks.*

EPICENTER

A town of dripping air conditioners, dust drifting—stinging gold in our eyes. We took our places for the relay, the ritual beginning—Albert down in the blocks for the start, me soaked in adrenalin in the second-leg zone, waiting for the baton to appear in my hand—a slippery tube of aluminum. Glint silver in transit. Butterfly nausea. Carry it home.

We were elegant in our motley regalia. Two streetwise islanders, a tall Icepick Slim—and a white boy wishing he was darker—all tugging at the elastic of our shining green shorts. We were pitted against hayseed drag racers and Italian orchard-owners' sons, homeboys fresh from the Homeless Boys Center and one crazed black greyhound with an evil blue eye.

We'd take the lead as soon as Albert stood up—a foregone conclusion—strained hamstrings and spit. Spiked shoes ripping up the packed dirt track. A rutted oval we were used to—none of that chic-tartan-spongy-black-asphalt for us.

Then the tremor struck, like the daydream-fear of my childhood—*in the Age of the Earthquake—look at the teacups.* At last—it's all going down.

The little town we were trying to run in, you see, had a precarious secret hidden underneath its fields and streets—under its gas stations and graveyard—under the cannery and the loading docks.

Heart stitched close, my shoes tied tight—lungs, groin and legs ready for the electrocution of speed—I watched the boys on the starting line poised on sprinters' tense thumbs topple over in unison.

Whistles blew, horns honked—false start! False start. No aftershock. No nothing at all. Just dust and silence in the bleachers—all of us holding ourselves to the ground, waiting for a total eclipse of the water tower, and the track to disappear down a golden angry crack in the world.

Finally, the whistles and the crowd and the teams breathed again. Someone who knew the eccentricities of the valley decided it was *all right.*

We'd run after all, it seemed. Knee to thigh in our narrow lanes, we'd stride along the fault line in the heat of the familiar sun in the middle of nowhere—and winning.

THE SHOVELER

It was 108 degrees Fahrenheit when my stepfather decided the rock beds circling our seven pear trees needed weeding. Better than that, he proclaimed that the stones should be levitated and polyethylene laid down to keep the weeds from growing back. Smart thinking.

So, I maneuvered that accursed sky-blue wheelbarrow fringed with rust to the base of the dry trees—plucked the shovel from the shed, dog shit still stuck to the edge—and began to toy with the stones, listening to them more than lifting them at first, ringing and plopping on the lawn.

The leathery golden pears fell all around me, bursting juice on the piles of stones I shoveled in a mist of perspiration until . . . I scratched my shoulder blade on one of the sharp branches . . . and looked up to see Gwen Janco watching . . . watching me . . . working without my shirt on beside the cardboard box wet with the mush of the ruined fruit.

Was it in your green eyes, Gwen? Or the way you wore your hair? It was something subtle—not your long body that had yet to fully blossom. But it was something sharp, too, like one of those stiff branches. A glance across dark noon summer space . . . and time.

The pears floating in the zero gravity of the still heat melted in midair, attracting yellow jackets, while I drove the bell of the shovel into the mounds, listening to them strike the crisp fresh-cut plastic. Gwen. Something we exchanged in that fascinated vacuum is still inside me. I catch a glimpse of it in tool shed windows and bathroom mirrors—especially on becalmed afternoons, when I'm drunk with loneliness, or mysteries about the past.

And there you are once more, as real as any moist lost July can never be. Green eyed and witnessing . . . watching you falling toward me, exploding sweetness, not another sound in the neighborhood. Not a car, not a spaniel—not even a hornet's wing. The girl I couldn't have . . . all mine. All me. Spray of fallen fruit on my bare chest.

VAT 69

I sort of remember the first time I ever got drunk. Mike and I sat against a sun-burnt brick wall, on a bed of broken glass ground into powder, and gulped down two fifths of Scotch in less than two minutes.

I don't remember much after that.

Except for some reason, falling face down on Angela Terry's bed.

I know well enough the reason why I fell. I was trying to touch one hand to the carpet to keep from spinning right out of the room, with the other hand smacked up against her bubblegum aqua wall, with a pink bra in sight, in the black behind my eyeballs little emergency lights that looked like the decals that parents used to stick in windows to tell firemen where the children sleep (back when people didn't worry so much about child molesters and suburban teenage vampires).

Then of course, I had to avoid the vomit on the bedspread and rearrange her stuffed animals. But how I ever got to the door, let alone inside of Angela's house, remains one of at least my life's great mysteries.

I wonder if I knew that the Terrys weren't home, or if I was just winging it?

That Airedale gave me some trouble, though. Good thing about her little brother's backyard trampoline.

Well, sort of a good thing. When the swelling went down.

AWAY GAMES

When I was little, I called it the Bighound Bus but I meant the mighty Greyhound. From Portland to the Port Authority, the cheapest distance between two points.

Too many is the number of nights I spent "riding the Dog" between the broken homes. I smelled the burgers sizzling, rolling into Morgan Hill at midnight, and the odor of toilets overflowing in San Jose. I saw the lingerie and violence of Oakland neon, the broken glass shining like broken glass in the street.

But I always look back to one Christmas Eve when I was riding with drunken soldiers smoking White Owl cigars—two hookers from Vallejo across the aisle, and a junkie beside me who was in a bad way all the way from the Fifth Ward in Houston.

A black woman rose with a bassinet she'd been balancing and when the bus stopped at a station, she stepped off for a moment—and I swear that when she came back, the bassinet was gone.

On the highway home from high school football games, I used to dream about that child. While the cheerleaders chanted in the back of the bus, I wondered what it would be like to grow up in the midst of smoke and baggage, the soft voices behind me singing . . . *Beat 'em bust 'em . . . that's our custom . . . roll 'em . . . roll 'em . . .*

DANDELION SAFARI

You could smoke dope in that savannah of gopher holes and garter snakes. You could spray the names of teachers that pissed you off on the windswept cinderblock walls.

Supposedly, the owner of the Lion Park once wore a pith helmet and even waved a whip to wake up the sleepy stars of his show, but the tourists never arrived in the droves he'd dreamed about, so he started missing his payments and hitting the bottle. Then he fell for the girl who worked the peanut counter, knocked her up and went down on statutory rape charges.

But she remained loyal . . . and one afternoon before the bank foreclosed, they made love in his Lincoln at the lights of the railway crossing . . . until an early evening express collided with the car and killed them both. Then men in a big truck from a zoo somewhere came to collect the animals orphaned by the accident. Some of those sad beasts had been waiting a long time for meat.

I don't know if we ever believed the story completely, but I can say for certain that when my friends and I wandered through the barren cages overgrown with grass and thistles, we always imagined we were being followed.

Whistling across the mouth of a brown beer bottle, we imagined we heard huge paws padding softly in the golden dry—or the light stride of a young girl's ghost.

It wasn't until we were staring at the red-eyed signal beside the tracks, where the accident was rumored to have occurred, that we relaxed—and even then, superstition claimed that it was good luck to place an empty bottle on the rails.

When the sun went down and the breeze began to breathe, you might've heard as many as twenty empty bottles blowing, like a phantom freight train closing in. We called it the ROAR OF THE IONS, just like the battered billboard by the highway promised us we'd hear.

LOS MURMURADORES

K*nee-deep in manure and mud.* Our arms ached with the weight of the irrigation pipes, our eyes drawn to the distant silver spindles spraying a fine mist of stolen water over green iceberg lettuce.

At dusk we'd gather around the cool blue rectangle of the ranch's pool just to listen to the hiss of the tile-cleaning jet, because swimming was tolerated only in the canal.

We all played Wiffle ball in our boxer shorts, and we all doused bullfrogs with lighter fluid. But when the kegs of beer were pumped, Stamond Jones, the foreman, allowed only the gringos to drink.

With cold foam in his belly, he ruled with a uniquely white blend of old-fashioned cruelty and a modern time-is-money lust for machines.

I remember the day he installed the automatic scarecrow to bedevil the magpies. It was a *self-contained, fully independent bird-scaring system,* he proudly informed us.

Whatever it was, it scared the tar out of the children who lived in the wetback hovels behind the fuel depot.

In California, they say when you walk through the orchards, someone's always watching you. But when you hear the peach trees whispering in fearful Spanish, you know you're being watched by the wide young eyes of the orchard itself.

INDEPENDENCE NIGHT

I met Lewis "the Dollar Bill" Hill, whose head shape reminded me of the Australopithecus robustus skull in my Life Nature Library book Early Man, *at a thing called Boys State.* It was a weeklong program at Cal State–Sacramento run by the American Legion to build character, inspire leadership, acquaint young men with the political system and, of course, develop teamwork. I was the only one at my school who came to the interview session, at the insistence of one of my teachers, who thought it would look good on my record. A sad little man with an American Legion T-shirt and a kind of a Shriner's hat (but not as good) was sitting all alone at a card table in the wrestling room of the gym. I told him I wanted to learn more about the political system and what made America a great country. That was in May. The program wasn't on until July.

I worked out in my mind that the only kind of guys that would go on something like that would be Eagle Scouts or namby-pamby nit-wits trying to garner another credential for college admission, which was exactly what I was doing. It never occurred to me that there'd be guys like me there. It didn't really occur to me that anyone was like me anywhere.

The weeks passed, I worked for a month in the fields and at last the bus came. Suddenly I was in Sacramento and it was about 200 degrees. I put on my white Boys State T-shirt that you had to wear. I found my room and started reconciling myself to a week of excruciating boredom and alienation. Then I heard a voice that made me stop unpacking my underwear.

"Look out, people, the Dollar Bill's doin' some serious inflation."

"Hm," I thought. I had my hash pipe in my hand at the time, which I carried everywhere just in case—and just when I thought I'd bury it for a week in a ball of socks—I had this feeling I might need it after all. I went out to have a look. A Neanderthal-looking black guy in scarlet gym shorts was in the process of inflating a green-and-yellow-spotted pool pony in the hall. I was pretty sure I knew where this particular pool pony had come from, having already inspected the swimming facilities. Some sort of children's summer swimming class was happening and pool ponies were standard issue. I suspected there would be one less pool pony come roundup time. I also suspected I was looking at one of my two roommates.

I was right. This figure, who kept referring to himself as "the Dollar Bill," was indeed one of my roommates and for reasons that remain obscure, he was attempting to see just how much air the rustled pool pony could hold. "Jesus," I said, "it's going to explode!" His face was swollen and his eyes were bulging and the spots on the pool pony were stretching out until they were fat blobs, the plastic skin as a tight as a drum.

I must've recognized a kindred spirit in his distorted face, because I had a sudden flash of inspiration. "Helium!" I shouted suddenly. "We'll send it up like a balloon!"

That got his attention. He checked me out with a quick street glance. "Well, *all right*. Now you're talkin'."

With all these guys in white American Legion Boys State T-shirts around, I was paranoid about talking about drugs or partying. We were there to learn. Then our third roommate showed up. His name was Jim. He was a Tex-Mex-looking guy from Modesto, which we didn't hold against him. He worked as a welder after school and he'd made enough money to buy an El Camino with a camper top and a mattress in the back. Jimbo's big thing in life was girls, which he called his "old ladies." That impressed me. He'd already bagged quite a bit of wild game and he came to study the democratic process with a Tupperware container of very fine sinsemilla, which we proceeded to torch in my pipe, while explaining our dilemma about getting some helium for the pool pony.

Substantial quantities of helium are readily available. It's after all the second most common element, and with Jimbo's background in welding, we thought we had a natural edge in locating some. It didn't matter. Lewis the Dollar Bill was on the case. While Jimbo and I and the rest of the Boys Police State trooped off to the basketball gym for an assembly where we were addressed by the little eighty-year-old head of the American Legion and unofficial mascot of the program, Philo, a bizarre white-haired man who stood only about four feet tall, Lewis was busy "borrowing" several helium cylinders from a nearby carnival that was gearing up to do a big balloon business on the Fourth of July. We'd set our minds on nabbing all the pool ponies and sending them aloft.

Jimbo, who had smoked about three bowls too many before going in, took one look at Philo and decided a cheer was in order. There were over a thousand guys in that gym. If you wanted a cheer to be heard, you had to stand up and stamp your feet. To the sheer amazement, amusement and shock of all of us around him, Jimbo leapt to his feet, and like a demented street corner evangelist screaming for the world to repent its sins and win one for the home team, he started clapping his hands, pounding his feet and bellowing, "Philo! Philo! Philo!"

The ferocity of his enthusiasm was intense. He seemed so happy, so sure he was doing the right thing—I couldn't leave him there, belting his heart out, alone. I jumped to my feet, for there was no slow rising—straight into it—born again—"Philo! Philo! Philo!"

By now there was a lot of commotion around the echoing gym. Little Philo was standing at half-court transfixed before a skinny microphone that was taller than he was. If he'd said anything into the microphone the cheer would've died. But he didn't. He must've been taken off guard—and I think his vanity was inflated. He stood stone still, soaking in this strange praise drifting down from the bleachers. Jimbo and I yelled on. "Philo! Philo! Philo!"

Suddenly, the boy next to me rose and joined in. "Is this what you do? Does this happen every year?" Not to be left alone, the kid slapped his friend next to him. He started cheering the loudest of all. Then across the arena a lone bug-eyed young scientist rose like the dead and started *screaming*. "PHILO! PHILO! PHILO!" Jimbo's voice was cracking with the strain and our hands were pain-red from clapping, but he stepped out of his seat at the end of a row and started gesturing to a whole section. He was getting some warped looks, but he was way past caring about that. He just swung his arms like a symphony conductor. It took ten seconds of the most committed crowd work I've ever seen. Finally, finally, they rose! And just as Jimbo triumphed over them, another whole section rose in unison, their feet thundering, their voices raised. Then another! "PHILO! PHILO! PHILO!" This was the real democratic process in action. Just shout loud enough and people will join in.

Down in the center of the court Philo stood, listening to his name screamed and chanted, and ever so slightly, almost invisibly, barely perceptibly, you could almost see his hands move, his shoe quiver. Suddenly Philo clapped and stomped his foot! The dam was broken! One thousand boys were on their feet cheering, "PHILO! PHILO! PHILO!" We'd turned a silly little white-haired elf into a hero—or at least a mascot.

While we were chanting and cheering, Lewis was stealing enough helium to set a whole box canyon of pool ponies aloft. Why send one, when you can send them all? The obvious occasion was the Fourth of July, Independence Day. There was going to be a full moon and fireworks over the river. What a way to be proud to be an American. So we broke into the swimming pool and heisted every single pool pony we could find. We were going to launch them from the roof of our dormitory at exactly midnight, having enjoyed the fireworks display stoned out of our minds. The only problem was we wanted something to drink too. That's what national holidays are all about, after all.

But to make a booze run, we had to cross a narrow bridge that passed through a huge cyclone fence marking the boundary of the campus. Jimbo had the misfortune of looking like a Mexican gang leader. Lewis's skull would've attracted attention in a museum of natural history, and I looked like I couldn't decide if I was a hippie or a pimp, with shoulder-length hair, mirror shades and a blue satin pool-shark vest. We'd stand out like dog's balls once we crossed the bridge. *But the most remarkable thing of all is that all three of us forgot to take off our Boys State T-shirts.*

The liquor store we went to was like a low-budget 7-Eleven with a cinderblock wall about knee-high surrounding the parking lot. Behind the store was an overgrown field that was waiting for the sprawl of housing developments to catch up with it. One street had been finished. Bulldozers, back hoes and steam rollers waited in the next cul-de-sac, then a dreadful high-rise of swinging-singles apartments.

Well, we were so high, it hadn't clicked yet that we were still wearing our "uniforms," which proclaimed to all the world that we were underage. So there we were, loaded down with enough booze to drown, when in walks Mr. Higginbottom, one of the dorm monitors, wearing his Boys State T-shirt and American Legion hat. He was about forty-five and one of the biggest tight-asses the world has ever seen. The burly pea brain with Clark Kent glasses behind the counter took one look at him and three looks at us, and noticed something similar, but he couldn't put his finger on it. He may have wondered about our ages, but we'd given him exact change. It was easier just to let us go. Lewis was out the door in a flash with a shopping cart filled with clinking bottles. Jimbo and I froze just long enough for Higginbottom to get a make on our T-shirts. Outside, Higginbottom's two buddies were in a car. I heard one of them call out to Lewis. I thought if we could just keep cool . . . Then the cashier blew it all by bolting out and hollering, "Hey, you forgot your tequila!"

A car door opened. Higginbottom ran out and yelled. Lewis was waddling at high speed behind the creaky-wheeled cart. Jimbo and I were right behind. Higginbottom got in the car. We heard him say, "Cut them off at the bridge; they're some of ours." Tires screeched. We were done for. Expulsion. Apologies to parents and principals. We'd already heard some of the horror stories. And what about our pool ponies, sitting up on the roof with all those stolen cylinders of helium? No, they weren't going to take us alive! We grabbed as many bottles as we could carry and bounded across that vacant field, laughing like idiots in our white T-shirts. The grass was chest-high. There were huge potholes. If we tripped and fell, a broken bottle might cut us open. Then they'd catch us at the bridge. If we could only slip back in, they'd have to pick us out of a thousand other guys in white T-shirts. We could disguise ourselves somehow. Once we were back on campus, we could hide the booze and they couldn't prove a thing. We *had* to make it to the bridge.

We were running and laughing through tall grass, racing a brown Camaro to a narrow bridge, and I don't think I've ever been happier. Even when I hit that gopher hole and flew ass-over-elbow with a terrible wrenching pain in my ankle, I was still laughing. I crashed in a heap of cement dust and dandelions. Jimbo ran on and made the bridge just as the brown Camaro skidded into the dirt beside the Cyclone fence. One safe, two still on the outside. One man down. Lewis, who ran like an electrocuted gazelle hallucinating cheetahs in every direction, froze in midstride, torn between helping me and saving his own ass. He had about a heartbeat to make up his mind.

I didn't know then that a year later, on my birthday, I'd drive my old Dodge Dart to pick Lewis up to go see an Earth, Wind and Fire concert at the Oakland Coliseum. Lewis lived in Richmond, a gritty shipbuilder's town of sheet metal and domestic murders, on the bad side of the Bay. It was a 1940s pink beaverboard bungalow that smelled of damp foam. Lewis let me in and I could see he was anxious to leave. We didn't quite get out in time. A black man about thirty-five, naked except for a dirty white tank top and a bandage on his foot, staggered out of one of the little bedrooms into the kitchen and took a leak in the sink. We heard what I took to be Lewis's mother croak out hoarsely from the bedroom. Lewis slammed the door when we left.

The concert was great but I only really remember two things about that night, other than the guy pissing in the sink. I remember having to wait two hours after the concert was over to find the car because we got so high I forgot where I'd parked it. And I remember discovering the next morning that I'd broken every finger in my right hand. How the fight started, I'll never know. I know I hit this big mother as hard as I could in the face. Somewhere in the fog I felt a hot freezing pain in my hand and I saw Lewis lashing out at my opponent with both fists flying. I'd hit the guy with all I had and he was still coming. If it hadn't been for Lewis I would've spent my birthday in the hospital. It's funny, because he always insisted that he didn't like white people. He liked to think of himself as blacker than black. "What about me?" I asked him as I drove him home that night. "You?" he said. "Well, in your case—I make an exception." I never did find out why.

But back at Boys State, Lewis dug in, spun on his heels, reached down and pulled me up and we dashed off toward the unfinished housing development. We'd missed the bridge but they hadn't caught us yet. Although my ankle ached like hell, we made it down the gravel road under the skeletons of young streetlights in the direction of the swinging-singles apartments, where it sounded as if a big party was in progress. The brown Camaro took off in hot pursuit. I had this sickening feeling we were going to play cat-and-mouse with those bastards. The sun was going down. Only a few more hours to Pool Pony Launching. We had to be there.

The apartment building had security doors, but fortunately the pool didn't. We snuck around to find one of the most humungous pool parties of all time—a perfect hiding place. Just mingle with the crazy natives and we'd be all right. You can show up anywhere with a bottle and be welcome. We had four bottles, two thumb-thick joints and a matchbox-size block of Lebanese hash. The people even liked our T-shirts. They thought it was a good joke! When Higginbottom and crew came around, we were hiding in the filter room with two gorgeous blondes. We danced, we partied. We might have stayed there all night, but we had an obligation to Jimbo to be on the roof of our dorm at midnight. So we at last decided to make a run for it, or in my case, a hobble.

An old Sam Cooke record was coming on when we split. We could hear the music drifting out over the desolate development as we stumbled down the dusty, unmade streets. "*We're having a party . . . everybody's singin' . . . dancin' to the music . . . on the radio . . .* " Pleasantly plastered, wandering through a haunted display-home village on a full moon Fourth of July night . . . imagine our surprise to see a brown Camaro waiting by the bridge.

"Fuckin' hell, man! Those dudes don't give up," Lewis moaned, his eyes wide with distress.

We hadn't expected they'd wait for us. It had been hours. More. It was almost midnight. We stopped and listened. We had another surprise in store for us. Higginbottom's Doberman. I don't know why they let him bring that vicious dog along with him for the week but they did. It was so well trained it was scary. The Doberman was outside the car, patrolling the bridge. I was a little sorry we hadn't robbed a few banks, given how serious these assholes were taking it. Now we were going to get ripped to shreds by some sicko attack dog that Higginbottom probably did obscene things to when no one was around. Our only choice was up and over the giant Cyclone fence that looked like some menacing industrial spiderweb. Above us the moon was full and huge. Between us and the assholes, a great soft willow tree. Without that, they would've seen us. We still had a chance.

But what about Jimbo? It was one minute to midnight. Had he made it safely back? Was he in place on the roof, anxiously awaiting our arrival? Or was he now sleeping like a stoned-out wimp, dreaming of his old ladies? Our answer came on the third or fourth stroke of midnight, which echoed out across the campus and the creek as we clung to the crest of the fence and swung our legs over. Lewis saw them first. Shadows rising toward the moon, drifting on a light breeze. First one. And then another. And another. *Pool ponies on the wing.*

"Reach for the Devil and howl at the moon!" said Lewis under his breath. "Have you *ever* seen anything more mighty than that?"

Jimbo had launched every single goddamn pool pony. They rose into the moonlight like creatures from another world. Higginbottom and his henchmen saw them too. For those few seconds hanging up in the fence with Lewis, I had a suspicion that great things were still possible.

I didn't know then that I'd never see Jimbo again after that week, despite all our plans—and of course I had no way of knowing that Lewis would one day become a cop of all things, and one night raid a crack house only a few blocks from where he grew up and get torn apart by some sonofabitch with an Ingram machine pistol, leaving behind a baby girl and a pretty wife.

But I don't think knowing would've made me cling any harder to those mesh diamonds as the pool ponies ghosted slowly over the river, Lewis singing softly, in spite of that damn Doberman, "*We're having a party . . .*"

Lewis died having been awarded the highest commendation for bravery in the line of duty that a metropolitan police officer can receive. He was just 30.

FOOTPRINTS IN A FIELD OF ASPARAGUS

I vaguely remembered arguing with the clown at Jack in the Box (something I've done on more than one occasion). But I definitely don't remember dying.

Still, it was dark all around, just the way I'd dreamed it would be.

Torrance had been driving . . . and we reached out to touch the dashboard, to see if things were still real . . . and yes, we were just as we'd been in life, when we'd been back on the highway. (High way is right.)

There was an eerie music filling the car—and we both said, "Where are we?" at the exact same time.

Judging from the damp peat that accumulated on our shoes the moment we stepped out of the car, we were in an asparagus field just outside Salinas . . . evidence of a nice lost-consciousness glide off the asphalt to avoid a State Farm Insurance billboard showing a pair of giant hands holding a bewildered white couple. This discovery prompted others.

The faintly celestial glow in the distance proved to be the Italian Villa . . . best pizza for miles. The music of the afterworld turned out to be Pink Floyd. I thought it sounded familiar.

I took the wheel to get us out of the mud, and Torrance slumped over in relieved disgrace, rolling a joint to calm his nerves. I had to admire the nodded-out swerve to avoid the billboard, though, even though I didn't recall it. Just looking at the tracks in the black damp earth told me we could've ended up in those giant hands at the speed we'd probably been going. But bigger hands were holding us.

After the trauma and dislocation of our little late-night field trip, I had the mistaken idea that we were indestructible and that the drive home would be easy and uneventful, once we made it back to the road.

But following the white lines again with great care, about two miles before our turnoff, I spotted a car coming toward us in *our* lane.

I started honking the horn like a madman, thinking, damn it, we'd just survived a field of asparagus and a tight corner. And the sun was starting to come up.

At the very last minute, the oncoming car jerked hard to avoid collision, me riding both the line and the shoulder, ready to head into whichever field lay open.

I watched until the sunrise took him in a ball of blood. A loner in need of a field of sleep—or some stoners out late like us, on their way to bed somewhere or headed all the way home.

CAHOOTS

My father got smashed at my high school's father-son athletic awards banquet. They'd organized predinner drinks for the dads and Dad got predinner drunk. He must've been drinking beforehand—I'd never seen him so incapacitated. His face was red and swollen, and there was a layer of sweat on it like the condensation on a block of cheese on a humid day. His breathing was heavy, his speech badly slurred, and in order to stay standing, he was forced to perform a kind of dance that brought to mind a cartoon character or a very bad actor in the early stages of what would be a long, drawn-out death scene.

When we filed into the cafeteria for the banquet, things got worse. There was a glass case full of sports trophies and a wooden signboard listing the school's athletic records down through the years. Dad slammed his shoulder against the side of the glass on the way past and a trophy fell over on the shelf inside. It could easily have rolled like a bowling pin and taken out the whole shelf—or the shelf could've broken. Or the glass door could've shattered. Fortunately, only a small wooden statue with a tiny gold cross-country runner tipped over.

Then Dad tipped over. And like the cross-country runner, frozen in midstride, he seemed both still and still moving on the floor—as if the change in elevation and direction hadn't registered. By this time, I could feel the eyes all over me. My friend Kyle looked at me with a grimace of apology. I had no idea what to do, except to get Dad on his feet, keep moving in line—get seated fast. Maybe some food would sober him up.

Some food! I sat him down at one of the long tables and told him to wait while I went to the buffet to fix his plate. I took my eyes off him for one minute—and then fear and embarrassment got the better of me and I looked back. He was gone. He'd gone around the other way, nearly pulling a tablecloth out from one setting and almost destroying the circular table that displayed the desserts. Then he found the plates. Everyone cleared away. I couldn't seem to move. All I could do was watch him go to work.

He plucked and picked and ladled and slathered—and piled and crammed and stacked and smushed. It was only when I thought he was going to keel over and take out the whole buffet that I regained control of my body. I got him back to the table with the help of Kyle's dad, losing dinner rolls and lemon-glazed carrots along the way. I was so angry, so ashamed. Yet I still thought that food would help.

The problem was that there was so much food on his plate, he couldn't eat anything without spilling some. Then more—and more. A revoltingly large slice of bloody roast beef fell in his lap and he didn't even notice. Peas tumbled, English mustard smeared. And the sounds he made. Johnny Johnstone and his father actually got up and moved to another table. Then suddenly Dad belched—an awful-smelling, resonant bark. His head lolled and he pitched forward into his plate, splattering mashed potatoes and gravy.

Someone at the table behind us laughed sharply. No one else said a word. The whole hall went silent, everyone looking at my father, who on my side appeared to be sporting a sideburn of tangy cheese cauliflower. Frances Perada, the sister of one of my friends, was serving drinks; she helped me get Dad out of his chair. The mashed potatoes made a muddy, sucking sound when we peeled him free. His suit was ruined. But Dr. Abrams was more worried about his breathing. We dragged him into the kitchen and laid him out on one of the long stainless steel bench tops, at the end of which were piled chicken carcasses and a mountain of moist potato skins. Dr. Abrams checked his airway and his pulse, and Frances helped me clean his face with a wet dish towel.

When he came around he needed to go to the bathroom. I carried him under the arms and walked him to the men's room like a piece of awkward furniture. Just in time. I pushed open the stall door and he started spewing. I was holding on to him but the force of the upchuck yanked him loose and he fell forward, smacking his head on the white ceramic tank, then bouncing back, clutching the toilet seat as if he were drowning in the floor.

We never went back to the banquet. It took me an hour to clean up the bathroom, Dad propped against the toilet in another stall, his forehead wrapped in a big moist turban of paper towels. My friends and rivals and their fathers came and used the facilities and left. Some asked quiet questions. Most, gratefully, did not. A couple of the other dads were tipsy, but nothing like this.

The thing I kept thinking about as I mopped up was that I'd been drunk myself only two nights before. Very drunk. In fact I was so drunk, when wandering back across the soccer field in the middle of the night, I blundered into the nylon net of the goal. I had no idea what it was—it was like some giant spiderweb set up there to trap me and I got hopelessly tangled. I finally blacked out and only woke up at sunrise, stiff and wet from the dew.

Now here was my father, leaning against a wall and smelling of puke. It would be another few years before he died, but I see now that I was witnessing a ghastly preview. Somehow, without warning, time had condensed around us. That was where the blood and bodily fluids came from. We'd been in an accident. A time implosion.

After Dad was emptied out, I endeavored to drive him back to his motel to sleep it off, but after great effort he managed to inform me that he hadn't come down alone. He'd brought Marti with him. She was back at the motel and he pleaded with me not to let her see him that way.

Marti was his "girlfriend" of the moment, but Dad was thinking meal ticket. She was a wealthy woman from Marin County, whose even wealthier husband had hanged himself. How she met my father I'm not sure. I don't know how Dad met any of his counselees. In any case, he started sleeping with her. (I think it would be safe to assume that he bedded the majority of the women he counseled. The men he got drunk with. A simple strategy.)

Dad had left his second wife and her kids (the family I'd come to think of as my own, after he divorced my mother) to be with Marti. Having been stuck in a combative marriage for twenty years, Marti was ready to kick up her heels. She had money, she had big tits, she had a lot of guilt and sadness. She wanted to have fun. To fuck. To travel. To escape. And nobody was better at escaping from responsibility than my father. So they were having a pretty good time. If only Dad could nudge her to the altar, his financial future would be set. No wonder he didn't want her to see him in such a condition.

But if he couldn't go back to the motel, that meant he had to come home with me. That meant smuggling him into my bedroom, because of course I couldn't explain things to my mother and stepfather. I couldn't explain anything to them. They already disapproved of Dad enough without seeing him stained and slurring.

I'd slipped out of my room and back into it in the wee hours many times before. But I'd never attempted so stealthy a maneuver with such a handicap. Worse still, my father's pathological optimism had given him the idea that I'd somehow forgiven him, and that we were old buddies again—partners in crime, tomcatting around. He became giggly and sentimental. I wanted to kill him. Especially when I had to shoehorn him through the window. I might as well have brought home one of the derelicts who sleep under the pier. At least they would've been quiet. I kept thinking my mother was going to wake up. I finally got him set up on the floor by my bed, windows open because of the smell. He was having a great time—like we were sleeping out in a tree house.

The thing that really pissed me off is that he kept calling me Cahoots. When I was growing up, we had these two Old West characters: Cahoots McCoy and his trusty sidekick Crusty Drifter. We made up stories about them when we were camping and fishing—driving up into the mountains to drop a line in the American River, hoping to hook a couple of steelhead and lay them in a bed of spitting bacon in Dad's old Klondike skillet. Sometimes he'd give me a shot of Jim Beam. He'd have a few swigs and tell me about the days of his boyhood, when giant timber wolves roamed Minnesota and his father would bring home a muskellunge and drink his homemade vodka and start talking in Swedish to people who weren't there.

My father had an encyclopedic range of faults, but he could make a warm can of Snappy Tom tomato juice and a thrown rod twenty miles from the nearest town seem like a stroke of good fortune—and there aren't many people like that left anymore. I'm certainly not one of them. I realized this watching him when he finally fell asleep. I didn't really know him. Yet there we were, in that room together. A small dark moment.

I managed to get him out of the house the next morning without my mother and stepfather finding out—but I almost had a nervous breakdown doing it. By that time the remorse had kicked in and he barely spoke. I didn't have a thought in my head as to what to say to Marti about where he'd been all night (which proved to be the beginning of the end for that relationship, although Dad, as always, was philosophical about the downturn). Thankfully, Marti wasn't in the motel room when we got there. She'd left a note saying she was walking along the beach. I left Dad to clean himself up and start thinking of excuses, and went off to find another stretch of beach where I could pull the car over and get some sleep. I was beat. He'd snored heavily during the night. I was sure Mom would hear it. Then when he stopped snoring, I was afraid he'd stopped breathing. I lay there in bed watching him, listening to the clock, until the sound got smaller and smaller. Sometimes he'd talk in his sleep. Once he called out a name, but I didn't recognize it.

FRESH MELON

It doesn't matter that her brother was a sadist with small animals and her mother wished I were as tall as the keyboard player, who later crashed into a cop car while stoned at the wheel.

It doesn't matter that her father came from Castroville, the Artichoke Capital of the World—or that he took up painting as a hobby and shredded a bouquet of yellow roses I sent one Easter, when I laughed at the quaint little owls his brush had deformed.

The only thing that seems important now is that she tasted like fresh melon sprinkled with salt.

She was the girl I'd been expecting—the girl of summer, the girl of my youth. The real deal.

So many lovers, even wives later, and it's still her I hope to feel, to smell—and I reach across the bed for her, knowing that she's only hiding, waiting to step from behind the curtain of a new name and embrace me for forever again.

MR. VERY LATE NIGHT

I know, I know—it's not the most creative handle in the world. Lame. Pathetic. But I had to have some kind of gimmick and I couldn't very well call myself something like Nick the High Priest of Soul, could I? Nick was black, after all, and a real, professional DJ with a genuinely soulful deep voice and worked for KSOL in San Mateo, a true, legit radio station that actually made money—a station powerful enough for us to hear loud and clear down in Sand City. He was my idol at the time and I needed to show some respect.

I'd thought about variations on Dr. Dark, but I didn't have the credibility or the confidence, not to mention any experience or technical smarts to pull even that off. So, when I got alone behind the mike, I got flustered. But my choice of "mask for the airwaves" may have had some truth in it.

As you've probably gathered, I'd developed a major drug and alcohol problem in those days. Still, I wasn't so stoned or drunk not to realize that I was just a jerk-off white boy in my last year of high school with no training in radio and no business working for an underfunded soul station one step away—one writ, one lien from being classed a pirate and not a "vital voice of a dynamic multicultural community." Maybe Mr. Very Late Night was dead on the money—of which, of course, there wasn't any. At least not for me.

Did you pick up that mention of Sand City? I bet you've never heard of it or think I'm making that name up. There's some truth in that too. Sand City is like a figment of the imagination of the California town of Seaside, which you may have heard of because it's right next to Monterey and its peninsula of wealth and golf courses. Carmel . . . Clint Eastwood . . . Arnold Palmer country. One curve of bayside highway away from cypress trees and millionaires.

Seaside isn't like that now and seriously wasn't like that then. In my day, it was where the black people lived. Hispanics. Islanders. It was the home of Fort Ord, once one of the biggest military bases on the West Coast. It was where the maids and gardeners who serviced the sprawling Pebble Beach estates took the bus home. It was where prostitutes worked out of massage parlors and the backs of tattoo joints—sometimes cars. It was where the drugs got dealt and shots got fired. Working girls from the Bay Area would come down on the Greyhound to do army paydays and weekends out of leopard-print-bedspread motels with names like the Sea Foam and the Bay Inn (no way out). There were turf wars where black, Guamanian, Hispanic, and Filipina hookers would openly duke it out on the pavement, while local pimps looked on, ready to unload if anything moved from the catfight to the knife blade.

To be sure, there were many working-class people of all colors—along with some old Italian couples who bolted their doors and pulled their shades down early—but there were many, many streets like those in Compton that have a first-glance look of calm and seeming prosperity—that could then erupt in gunfire out of a single sweep of headlights.

Those living in the fog and ice-plant clapboard comfort of Pacific Grove or grotesque Del Monte Forest Tudor mansion extravagance would've looked hard for a twenty-four-hour pharmacy nearby in those days. They'd have had to drive to Seaside—and I bet they still do. Liquor stores, dark women, China White. Certain things just sell themselves and folks come hunting. When I knew the place, there was never a night when there weren't pimp-mobiles and lowriders cruising . . . white people on the prowl . . . searching . . . magnetized whether they knew what they were looking for or not. It was, simply put, East Oakland on the beach. And the strip of beach that bounded the highway, where Fremont Boulevard flowed down out of the fried chicken and burger joints, the panther girl motels and checks-cashed pawnshops—that was Sand City. Blink and you'd miss it. But in some places, you just know to keep your eyes open.

An abandoned army rifle range . . . the ruins of the White Surf Drive-In, the screen long collapsed or washed out to sea, only a few of the speaker poles remaining, buried in sand . . . and a complex of khaki green Quonset huts from World War II days that an enterprising former bodyguard, dope dealer, community organizer and failed Burger King franchisee named Brock McDaniels had peddled into some bleary-eyed semblance of a marginally real commercial radio station on the back of a government grant and a whole lot of chutzpah—that was the Sand City I knew.

How I got the late-night radio gig is a very long story that involves fried chicken, a failed dope deal and a night with a hooker, trying to prove I was a man. I don't think I need to go into all of that. The only thing I'll say by way of explanation is that I was then on the surface an honors student . . . with a stepbrother I loved who'd turned into a major car thief and who I'd crossed some lines with myself, jeopardizing my whole brilliant career. The kicker was, not only am I the son of a minister, but I come from a long line of religious people. And I don't mean just religious; I mean famous evangelists, who could pack tents and churches from Boston to Minneapolis via Alabama. My great-grandfather was enshrined like a conquering hero by the Baptist Society.

Still, the pure and the tainted are ever close. I first went out exploring in Seaside not to be another white boy looking to buy drugs. I went to sell them. I had attitude, even if I couldn't think of a very good name to call myself when a half-assed dream opportunity came my way. I wasn't expecting my dream to come true—I didn't even know what it was. That's one of my points, by the way. Maybe if you know what your dream is, it actually might become real, for a moment at least.

I only got the gig because Brock couldn't find anyone stupid enough to work those hours—he'd called all his markers in—and in order to maintain funding and keep his broadcasting license, some kind of programming had to be offered in that time slot. So, for the prince of darkness sum of $10 each shift, and maybe a napkin of sticky spare ribs, little white me got the chance to be something like a DJ on a black radio station one night a week, in the graveyard hours, playing records, thinking I was someone. The only person I told was my girlfriend Sal, who I'd picked up when my main squeeze, who I used to wait for on Pine Street in Salinas in the rain, dumped me because her mother came on to me when we were all drunk one night and I'd nodded out on their back summer porch after the county fair, when the mayor rode into the rodeo grounds on a buffalo and the beast got spooked by fireworks and stampeded through a cotton candy booth. After six Schlitz tall boys, how was I to know whose tits I was feeling? But it didn't look good when the girlfriend found us in the morning, I admit. I'm just glad her father Roy wasn't there to see too.

Anyway, of course I had to keep my parents—my mother and stepfather—fooled, sneaking out when they thought I was in bed. I was after all, Mr. Very Late Night.

Sal was known by many of my male friends as a slut. She may be the only true nymphomaniac I've ever known. She needed it constantly—and would finger herself on our drives to places like the Boardwalk in Santa Cruz. But she was also the kindest person I've ever known. A teenage alcoholic worse than I was, she'd had some sort of terrible life in her childhood, which she could never talk about even when crying—until she'd been adopted by a very wealthy judge and his wife. They were old for parents and lived in one of the monstrosities of Pebble Beach luxury that I mentioned earlier. One night, when Sal and I had been making out at Fanshell Beach, thinking the parents were gone, we drove back to her house to go hog wild.

We found the place entirely lit up and Perry Como on peak volume. Her mother was back east—but the judge had come back early from his conference in L.A., knocked down a full bottle of twelve-year-old Scotch and then hanged himself above his pool table with what looked like a throw line from a sailboat. Made me think back to my mother's uncle and that hay hook somewhere lost in time in Upstate New York . . . and the reason Marti had been getting "counseled" by my father. (I didn't tell you that the girlfriend before Sal, who tasted like salt and melon . . . whose dim-witted brother like shoving firecrackers up cats' butts and whose father was a fireman who got into a punch-up with me in their driveway once late at night when he caught me siphoning his gas tank so I could get home and have another fight with my stepfather for being so late . . . her name was Marti too. Unusual name for a girl. It's strange how things connect in life . . . in death.)

To make a long, brutal-soft story short, Sal broke as many windows of that great house as she could with the billiard balls and then fucked me in the room next door with Perry Como still on full bore. There's no other polite way to put it. It was a night and an accident that you couldn't just walk away from. I have a hard time explaining what it's like having sex with a girl when her adoptive father is suicidally silent in the next room, so I won't even try.

The next night, I had my show. My chance. My little moment at the mike. The thing I lived for then.

I didn't think I was going to make it. I was all swept up in the bizarreness and tragedy of the dangling judge, his toes inching the billiard balls, me and Sally screwing in the next room—or me trying, actually getting inside her and coming anyway—Sal coming too in a fit of anguished release and tears . . . all the doors and windows in that big house open or smashed, the smell of the sea . . . night shore mist drifting inside the house, mingling with the dead man's last cigar smoke.

It got right on top of me and I drank a bottle of vodka alone in my room, falling off the balcony sneaking out, almost spraining my ankle—then swerving through the forest nearly hitting a deer with the Isley Brothers' "Harvest for the World" at max volume, all my windows rolled down, hotboxing a Newport, sheets of term papers and Taco Bell wrappers blowing out onto the road like bits of scarecrow stuffing I could no longer contain.

Remarkably, I made it to Sand City with only one unplanned lane change.

But my mood didn't lift as it usually did when I got into what we called the canary seat. Brock, the heavily leveraged station owner, my boss and sponsor, was there with his girlfriend Charlene, getting high with Little John. (Brock was actually living in the studio illegally at the time because he couldn't pay the rent on his apartment and was about to lose his car. Of course he was there.)

Brock got higher than you would believe—and I don't blame him. You might too if as many people were chasing you for money. I said hey and went in to do my show, popping a benny I'd traded to the Weasel, Little John's brother, for a lude from the show before. The last thing I needed then was a downer. For people who like to drink, uppers are the only way to go. Before my crystal meth days, I went with as pure Benzedrine as I could get—black beauties in a pinch (Biphetamine). I liked to break the capsules open, razor clear the powder and snort it, wishing it was cocaine. Drugs had better names in those days. White crosses, yellowjackets, redheads, blue velvets. Always reminded me of the names of my father's fishing flies, which he tied by hand before he got the trembles.

I've never subscribed to that nonsense about not mixing drinks and drugs and proceeded to hit my stash of Jim Beam under the console, adding it to black coffee, waiting for a second wind from the speed while I played some Al Green and then James Brown's "Cold Sweat." I got sort of blurry and sloppy for a bit and then the crank kicked in. It was what we called a Rooster, one of the homemade brands of white lightning amphetamine cooked up by the greaser biker gangs in the valley.

Pretty soon I had a neck full of needles and was on a roll until I made the mistake of playing Isaac Hayes's version of "Walk on By," which got me thinking of my stepbrother again and the night the cops did us in the parking lot outside Solomon Grundy's at the Berkeley Marina (they made a great black bean soup at that restaurant, and when the pot smoke cleared, I could smell it in the fog coming in when the uniforms shook us down about the stolen motorcycles . . . little did I know how seriously his crime wave had really escalated). That was the song that had been playing when we got thrown down on the hood and cuffed. Such sadness on top of Sal and the billiard-ball-broken windows uneased me into murky psychic terrain.

All these crises I'd been party to but had managed to wriggle out of when others hadn't. What the hell was I doing with myself, ripped to the gills out at some sand-dune chicken-wire dope-haven excuse for a nada black radio station when I should've been home asleep getting ready for exams and real life? I was virtually the only white person who ever walked into that dismal set of Quonset huts with the stink of seal shit and dead seaweed all around—and certainly the only one who didn't have a felony conviction—and I was working on that.

On the wall in front of me was a list of emergency phone numbers . . . a pinup of a sizzling chocolate chick with a big bubble ass . . . a poster for the Monterey Jazz Festival . . . a flyer about a rally for farm workers' rights . . . a thumbtacked, faded and creased $50 bill that had on it in smeared felt pen the number of a call girl famous for giving great head before she OD'd. I felt the ghosts all around just like the fog.

Something odd and unprofessional, even unnerving happened then. Metaphysical, I hate to say. I had on the Five Satin's classic "In the Still of the Night," because I was feeling nostalgic, simultaneously hyped and burnt out, drunk yet wanting more drink—but on the other, off-air studio turntable, I had going a very obscure version of "Amazing Grace" by Blind Jack Wallis, essentially an old black hobo with a good voice, who died on the trolley line down in Memphis one rainy night long before I was born. It's a take like you've never heard on that famous song. He's not singing about something he's found—he's out there looking for it, clawing for it, pleading for it. It sounds like it was recorded in an asylum or an emergency room. He at one point just frankly screams.

Well, somehow (possibly because I was smashed) the broadcast feed intermingled the two songs on air to astonishing effect—at least to me. I was suddenly seized by some spirit of rebellion and reprieve. Both songs ended in perfect synch and I was left with empty space. Nothing planned, no neat transition. So, I improvised. I just started talking. Or rather . . . testifying. As I've said, I come from a crooked line of men of the cloth, some who died in rags, and for whatever reason I started witnessing . . . with some unexpected conviction . . .

> I am the Sinister Minister of the Meta-Midnight Chapel . . . a benign sign for those over the line. I am the leader and the breeder of the Choir of Ghosts gathered by the river of streets and the streets of casual slaughter. I am the Prophet of Loss and the Keeper of the Flame in the Rain . . . a fast passing light on the Coast Starlight train. I'm a preacher and a screecher and a graveyard shift teacher. Whoever is near to me better stay out of my way. Whoever is far . . . better come close. So you can hear me whisper of time and the blood and the family of orphans . . . and the Fire Road forward to the home you've never known—the long burning highway to the place of peace you've yet to find . . . but will . . . in me.
>
> Put your hands on the radio people . . . and be healed. All will be revealed. If you're at the end of your rope, don't give up hope . . . I'm at the end of your dial . . . and I've run the dark mile. Not a cigarette butt falls that I don't hear. I know what you fear . . . and how you can be free. Put your hands on the radio and your faith in me. We'll get through this night together. One step closer to a morning we want to remember. Behold, I am with you always . . . even unto the first rays of dawn.

For those of us on the edge, Today is now and we're doing all right.

So sayeth . . . Mr. Very Late Night.

Well, I was so mushed and wired I didn't know exactly what I'd said, but I knew I'd had to say it—and that it meant something. I think. Maybe it was my twisted nod to my father's or my great grandfather's famous sermons. Maybe I was just very high. Whatever. What the hell—I felt I was among real family . . . or all alone (which hopefully, when you think about it, is the same thing). Beyond the music I blasted, the silence was usually deafening by that hour. Who was out there listening really anyway?

Hmm. Well, I found out. Within two minutes of my impromptu homily, I thought the broadcasting authorities were running a raid on the station—or something worse. I half suspected some drug-related neurological crisis. The whole dashboard (that's what we called the switchboard) started lighting up like a pinball machine. Not that there were hundreds of lines, but still—soon every single light was bleeping and the phone was ringing.

Brock came bursting in from having been banging Charlene in the control room. He smelled openly of pussy and barbecue, with Kool cigarettes spilling out of the pants he was trying to pull up. "What the fuck you done, boy?" he yelled. "Answer that damn phone!"

So . . . I answered the calls. And found another world. Of soiled angels and shining devils . . . the bored and the belligerent . . . only the lonely and the undefeated . . . memories of the dead and requests for the loved . . . soldiers and security guards . . . a black cop going off duty . . . a Samoan baker just coming on . . . working girls and the permanently unemployed. I realized that there really had been an audience out there, just waiting to be tapped. Waiting for a change. Something different.

Over the course of that night I spoke to people too drunk to talk, who wanted to talk anyway. There were prayers for mercy, pleas for money and blessings, offers of money and blessings, people high out of their minds—and people just out of their minds. But there were others too: a priest who couldn't sleep, a trucker passing through on the way to Hayward, a gas station attendant in Soledad . . . the Mexican dishwashers at Golden West Pancakes. Late at night or early morning, I'd never really known how far the station's signal reached—and that's maybe something for us all to think of in our own ways. The revelation was amazing to me.

Forget good grades or applause on stage, or cheers when you score a touchdown—I was suddenly, directly in touch with not just an audience, but a congregation. A congregation of strangers maybe, but my people. I'd put my finger straight on a vibrating harmonic nerve of the red taillight central coast California vampire redemption hour. For the next hundred minutes I raved—off the top of my head. I preached, I sang, I mixed—I made a mess of the record library and spun for all I was worth. I did everything I could think to do with that studio until the first blue light outside began to bleed. I took calls from motel desk clerks, nurses, ambulance drivers and an all-night pizza joint. It was the best morning of my life and the sun hadn't even come up yet.

As much as I'd loved doing the show (and needed it) before then, that outburst was a turning-learning point. I don't know how it happened—but I was going to go with it. Without a conscious plan, I changed the format of my segment entirely, and the orientation of the station at large, in my own humble way. I still played music . . . and a much wider range than ever . . . soul, R&B, funk, jazz, gospel, novelty records . . . Kerouac and the Beats . . . old doo-wop. But I made a point of extended phone calls broadcast live.

Sometimes people spoke entirely in Spanish and I had only a dim idea of what they were saying. I talked with hookers and drill sergeants, dopers and doughnut shop waitresses. I made up my own ads for places that I liked and just threw them out . . . Orange Julius on Ocean Avenue in Carmel . . . Pioneer Ribs in Seaside . . . Golden West Pancakes in Pacific Grove (order the waffles and tip Jose well). Some of these establishments actually started to openly sponsor Brock and he couldn't have been happier—but I wasn't in it for the money—I just pushed places and people that I believed in. I hounded the benefits of soft water to plug my friend Mike's dad's business. I told people what service stations were open late. I gave major time to the Stop-Go market out on the River Road in Salinas where they still sold cold milk in real glass bottles, very good for calming your stomach on the way to meet a girlfriend with a violent father . . . along with Schlitz tall boys for afterwards. I told the local late night world about the backroom gambling that no one was supposed to know about at the Italian Villa, a cinderblock bunker between two spinach fields . . . and no big guys with five o'clock shadow came for me—instead I got a tub of carbonara and a bottle of Chianti delivered by cab.

I played Curtis Mayfield, Miles Davis, Parliament Funkadelic, Mary Wells, The Whispers, Major Lance . . . and Merle Haggard. A surprise in every box.

I resurrected our family's old story records and opened with "The Headless Horseman Song"—and I fleshed out the ghostly jamboree concept with regular spins of "The Monster Mash" . . . haunted house sound effects and snippets of the Mormon Tabernacle Choir. What's more, I pulled out the God trick that my sister had showed me when we were kids, of playing the voice of the Swordfish on *Bozo the Clown Under the Sea* on a different speed.

My whole sense of protocol shifted, as I read poems by Langston Hughes and Robinson Jeffers . . . and every time did another few sections of Steinbeck's *Tortilla Flat*, mixing in Sun Ra, Millie Jackson, Booker T. & the MG's, Oscar Brown Jr. and Gil Scott-Heron. But I always allowed plenty of time to talk to people, whether they were calling from Big Sur or Chualar—the Presidio or Alisal.

My parents never knew—but I talked to the night. We had open debates about police hassles . . . discussed the logistics of moving irrigation pipes in lettuce fields and the stench of the sugar beet refinery in Spreckels. Financial assistance was organized for a single mother of three in Marina, who'd had her nose broken and teeth knocked out by her deadbeat husband, who'd fled back to Kentucky. We found a Guatemalan woman a job as a housekeeper on the Seventeen Mile Drive . . . a teenage girl in Monterey named Venezuela decided to keep her baby . . . and a man (who turned out to be one of my teachers) anonymously confessed his love for teenage boys and how the stifling of his attraction had led him to become an alcoholic. I spoke to Prunedale and Moss Landing . . . itinerant pickers in Gonzales, insomniac, washed-up celebrities in Carmel Valley . . . students at Cabrillo College . . . janitors at the Navy Postgraduate School.

With my secret after-midnight identity consolidated, it naturally started to leak out a little. Especially when I was granted another night with a slot twice as long. I became something of a hero to Doc and Mike and my other insider friends at school. Outside this inner circle, people listening to me wondered what I looked like . . . how old I was . . . what kind of car I haunted the highways with when I wasn't the voice in the night-becoming-day. I developed a running gag about the town of Pismo Beach (where my character was supposedly from—don't know why, just came to me). I relentlessly harped on the quality of the ice water served at the Wagon Wheel Steakhouse in Carmel (late night summons forth the ironic as well as the sincere) and I had regular raving conversations with a Seaside pimp named Lebris, who drove a fire-orange diamond-in-the-back El Dorado (with two missing hubcaps) and was known for having fat girls in his stable. He'd sit on the hood of his ride by the pay phone outside the Chicken Shed drinking Colt 45 Malt Liquor. I once freaked him out by getting him live on air singing along with "People Get Ready." He actually had a really good bass tenor.

I lived for those few hours each week in that smelly room down on the drowned-body, otter-stiff beach. I was the howling-dog-hours minister of Fremont Boulevard. (Today, not one sign of that old dereliction remains. The shooting range has been reclaimed as beach . . . the empty industrial buildings have either been bulldozed or renovated and now house some kind of "artists' colony" . . . all of the speaker poles that used to stand like grave markers from the White Surf Drive-In have long been removed.)

Once Fort Ord closed down, everything changed. The Chicken Shed, Cash for Trash and several notorious motels are gone. I doubt you'd see a streetwalker in tiger skin shorts and six-inch heels on a summer night or find it as easy to score smack at 3 AM anymore. I guess you'd call that progress. I guess.

The rest of that school year, my last days of high school, passed in a blur. My gal Sal had a breakdown after her old man's exit and was sent off to some cooldown place in Santa Barbara. I think it was really an expensive rehab facility. I wouldn't see her again until the night of my eighteenth birthday, one of the few I remember in my life, when she took me out to the Sardine Factory restaurant on Cannery Row and we were served by a waiter with an eye patch. It was the first time I'd ever been out with a girl at a fancy place—and she paid. It was beautiful and harrowing because neither one of us could get past the image of her adoptive father's suspended sentence over the green felt . . . with all the curtains billowing, us in the other room with Perry Como. We just kissed goodnight afterward and I left town for the summer. And I'd never see her again except in dreams.

Surprisingly, you might say, given the stuff I was up to, I continued to do well in school all that last year. I won the English and drama prizes and a host of national awards. I blitzed the SATs. On paper I looked pretty good and received full scholarships to all the colleges I applied to: Amherst, Dartmouth, Harvard and Northwestern. I don't know why I didn't think of Yale or Princeton. I was all over the place—having accepted early admission to Amherst and then canceled. When the radio station deal had started, it kind of eclipsed all my normal thinking. I started believing I could actually be a radio personality like Nick the High Priest of Soul. I could become more magical . . . more late night. Like Wolfman Jack with fifty thousand watts of Soul Power and a border-blaster signal. My voice in the darkness got me thinking more about going into drama. (I heard someone talking about the dramatic arts one day and I thought they said "traumatic arts"—it seemed appropriate.) So, the plan come graduation day was to go to Northwestern (another dream that wouldn't come true). Who really knows what they want to be when they grow up, until it's too late? Not even Mr. Very Late Night could give you the answer to that mystery.

But sometimes still . . . all these years later . . . in that deeper dark just before morning somewhere alone, I think of Sal and Brock again . . . and I hear Mr. Very Late Night—just as I used to on the headphones when the sea mist was thick around that old tin shed. The signal's strong . . . finding me on one of the unofficial frequencies.

And he says, "*It's never too late if you can hear my voice.*"

EVERCLEAR

The summer I left home I spent a hot, weird month alone in a little desert crossroads called Searchlight, Nevada.

I lived in the shell of an old camper blistered with bass and trout decals. My neighbor, a retired postmaster from Needles, California, fired his shotgun every morning and would invite me over for a cold Olympia beer and thimblefuls of Everclear when the wind rose at dusk.

His name was Alf Milligan, but the reason why he sticks in my mind is that he had a remarkable collection of wanted posters that had filtered through his post office over thirty years. I couldn't help but think of Gus Gus.

In the evenings, we'd shuffle through those fugitive faces, some of them famous, some of them dead or apprehended—some still at large, living in somebody's storm cellar in Illinois, or in a crumbling bungalow on a back street of Veracruz.

There's nothing quite like those posters—with their cryptic, ominous remarks. *Travels under the alias of . . . has been known to wear a beard . . . last seen in Tucson.*

Alf's probably gone missing himself now.

Like a lot of desert people, he had a fond belief in life on other planets.

"Who knows," Alf said, "maybe somewhere out there, there's a kind of a small town with something like a post office in it—and in that post office there's a poster with a face on it that looks mysteriously like you or me."

He'd lick the Everclear from his lips and chase it with a swig of beer, reaching for a shotgun shell with a bright, strange look in his eyes, as if he expected he would one day visit such a place.

The last day I ever saw him, we collected all the wanted posters and let them loose. A dust devil swept them up over the mesquite. Lost faces. Some still wanted, some forgotten—fugitives in the fugitive wind.

FOREVER MINE

I got a tattoo on my nineteenth birthday. I figured I was old enough to get one and I was definitely still young enough to dream of waking up one twisted dawn in Singapore or Copenhagen and looking in the mirror and remembering the wasted golden days of my youth.

I started thinking about the tattoo the moment I arrived in L.A. I visited Cliff Raven's studio. His specialty was Oriental design, but a tiny black unicorn, beautifully detailed, would've cost me about four months' rent. I put the idea on a back burner until the afternoon of my birthday, when I found myself drifting around Hollywood, pleasantly pickled with my friend Matt Bauer, a would-be pro baseball player addicted to painkillers.

Mad life was streaming by. Huge fat Hispanic ladies screaming at their husbands, grotesquely powdered Jewish ladies arguing with shop assistants, car horns honking, music thumping, black kids dancing for money, cute little blondes in cut-off jeans, gays with their shirts off, old Italian men talking with their hands, old hippy ladies talking to themselves, Japanese tourists blinking in the sun after seeing *Deep Throat* a second time—a man in a straw hat talking about God, the Devil and retiring to Arizona.

Bauer kept saying it was important that I do something significant for my birthday. I told him about the tattoo idea. He became obsessed. I tried to fend him off. When it came down to it, I was a little nervous. He kept at me. Finally, we came across this place called the West Coast Tattoo Studio. Bauer said it was now or never. I said I had to find the right tattoo. Bauer asked what I had in mind. I thought for a second, and figured that a clown was a pretty unlikely design for them to have. And it couldn't be a wimpy clown. It had to be cool, like one of those old circus posters. It had to have a certain look, a certain expression—it had to capture that vanished-sideshow, ghost-carnival feeling. I said, "I'll do it, if I can get a clown tattoo." Bauer slapped me on the back.

The place was up on the second floor in a window overlooking the street. I don't know what I was expecting—some big, bearded fellow chewing Red Man tobacco—a lot of skulls and rebel flag designs in glass cases on the dirty walls.

What we found was a cross between a Sam Spade–type office and a veterinarian's. A Korean-looking guy without a shirt on was working on a longhair's forearm—putting the finishing touches on a coiled rattlesnake. The inker was locked in sweaty concentration and his own chest and back were entirely covered with an elaborately detailed series of dragons, imperial warriors, winged horses, naked women, and suns with fiery faces.

The next customer, or patient, was a vaguely Latina woman who lay back on a vinyl seat with her pants down and her you-know-what right up in another tattooist's face while he gave her a bright pink strawberry just above her pubic hair. His back was to me. He had a hatchet-head and a white T-shirt with huge sweat stains under the arms.

The third tattooist looked like a skinhead version of Richard Chamberlain. He was wearing a white cotton madras shirt that disguised but didn't hide the most disturbing tattoo I've ever seen. Fortunately, he didn't show it to me until after mine was done, or I'd have chickened out. I was plenty ready to chicken out and of course I had my excuse all ready—they didn't have the clown face I wanted.

Skin Man listened to my description, scowled and lit a cigarette. He pulled a ring binder off a shelf and flicked the pages. He stopped, then showed the page to me. It was *exactly* the face I had in mind. I looked at Bauer, who grinned hugely. Skin Man said, "The colors will fade a little in time, but when you die they'll be nice and bright again."

I didn't know what to say to that. I took off my shirt and Skin Man traced the outline from the stencil. The humming, sewing-machine irritation was just enough to keep me alert. Bauer went over to chat up the strawberry girl while I sat observing the swarming little dramas of Hollywood Boulevard unfold.

What I became fixated on was a wino—at least I thought he was a wino—lying motionless in the doorway of the International House of Pancakes across the street. I concluded later that if he was a wino, he was a fairly well-to-do one, because at first he had on a green fedora, a herringbone jacket, burgundy polyester trousers, white leather loafers and pale pink socks. It was a bright, warm afternoon, thousands of people in the street. This guy was lying down in the doorway of a popular restaurant and people were stepping over his body to get in and out. Hundreds more were stepping past him every minute.

I looked away to ash my cigarette and when I looked back, his green fedora was gone. I turned away to answer Bauer—for a split second—and the guy's shoes were gone. I thought I was seeing things. He was being picked clean and it was happening before my eyes. The crowds kept churning past. Then I lost sight of him again—and when he reappeared I got a glimpse—the guy was barefoot!

Finally, I watched an actual derelict steal the man's coat. It was done cleanly, but not so fast that it couldn't be seen by me, and about five hundred other people. I didn't see who got the trousers. Bauer came over after the strawberry girl left, and I got distracted. When I looked back the man was lying in a short-sleeved shirt and a pair of boxer shorts. I couldn't believe it. I didn't even notice that my tattoo was finished.

As if to welcome me to the fold, Skin Man took off his shirt. His chest was white, surprisingly delicate and hairless. Then he slowly turned to show us his back, which was entirely taken over by an enormous octopus—something out of an opium nightmare—Bosch meets an old Dutch map. The sheer intensity of the thing made me cringe. In each tentacle was a sword or an axe or—something. There were mermaids crushed in the grip of the suckered arms, black ink rising—sailors' knots, sunken ships, skeletons and sharks.

"It took seventy-five hours," he said without emotion. I nodded. He nodded. I paid and we left. We looked in a couple of store windows and watched this guy performing on the corner. He must've had double-jointed jaws because he was able to open his mouth, or what seemed like his whole head, just like a Pez dispenser. Anyway, by the time we got over to the IHOP, an ambulance or the cops had taken the guy in the doorway away. Completely gone. The slow fade finally finished.

It was frustrating because Bauer hadn't seen the guy from the window and hadn't really believed me when I told him what had been going on. What could I say? The mysterious thing is that later, whenever I tried to point out the West Coast Tattoo Studio to anyone, I could never find it again. It seems to have vanished off the face of the earth. No one even remembered where I thought it had been.

Of course I only have to roll up my sleeve to prove that at least for one warm afternoon, it existed. No matter if I wake up in Singapore or in the doorway of an International House of Pancakes. Even when I'm gone, the glitter in the clown's green eyes will still be bright. Skin Man told me.

THE RETURN OF THE SWIMMER

Now let me tell you about the water.

It was cold, a mountain lake a mile across beneath a granite ridge that ran like a serrated spine above the tree line.

Even in summer, the lake was immune to sunlight. The basin was pure glacial damage filled by waterfall straight from peaks of perpetual snow. It was a world made of words like *moraine* and *feldspar*, where the wind spoke pidgin Aspen, but very fluent Ice.

Sitting in an aluminum rowboat filled with pale green frogs that keep sliding down the slippery sides, you can feel the cold conducting through the thin metal, even in the squinting weather of full noon.

You might be curious about those frogs, but right now you are watching the water, watching the shore. You are waiting to initiate a rescue or to witness a Return.

An Easter morning in Minnesota spawned this, perhaps my father's strangest, obsession.

The day he turned eighteen was Easter Sunday. He left the church still singing hymns, and on a bet, he swam four miles across a lake he'd intended to walk around.

The war came and he came home wounded and that cold lake

bloomed ever brighter in his mind as the exact home of his elusive youth.

Twenty years and forty-five pounds later, he came upon another lake and became convinced that if he could swim across this body of water and back, he could regain the power and the purity of the day he swam with the hymns in his head, his friends on snowshoes, shivering in a cloud of shoreline anticipation.

In the blinding benediction of noon he'd start—splashing water down his trunks, behind his neck, underneath his arms. Then he'd dive and shiver in a body-wide spasm and begin the slow pilgrimage with his precise scissors kick. Incantatory Swimmer. He swam like a man Released.

I kept pace with him through the liquid ice, wondering all the while what he was thinking of as he swam away from himself, deep into Rhythm. Was it hymns like "Oh Beautiful Upon the Mountains?" The girls he might've married? The sons he might've had?

I think now it was raw youth for the losing he pursued—the soul cinnamon of childhood, his dead war buddies—his young animal grace turned to flab and angina. He would will it all back, or swim to where it still existed . . . and I would follow him straight up the waterfall if need be—in my silver ark of frogs.

Then he decided that having me row beside him was cheating. There was no rescue boat on that morning in Minnesota. So he made me wait with binoculars while he went the distance alone.

Despite everything I knew to be true, I always believed that somehow, *this time* I would peer through the field glasses and find my father churning back, transformed by the Distance. He'd rise from the water a young man, fresh with the supernatural blessing of second-strength and virility.

I'm here to tell you that magic is cruel. The last time he attempted the crossing, I barely got to him in time. His body was blue. He had trouble getting in the boat. His lips were swollen—heart palpitating, limbs leaden, speech incoherent. We took him to the hospital. He caught pneumonia a week later and the antibiotics mixed badly with his booze.

Wait 'til next year, I tried to reassure him. But the last three horrific years passed and he died in his chair watching a rerun of *Bonanza*.

He never returned to that lake of time and spirits. But I did, and through him, to the earlier lake of his youth.

I became acquainted with the friends who stood on the freezing shore that Easter. I became familiar with my own fierce impotence—the death grip that begins in childhood, the hunger of love and instinct that creates substance by the strength of its longing.

Now I find, I too need to swim across cold water alone. In my mind I must be swimming to meet him—swimming to be him. You see, we do return—by son, by ghost, by God—you have returned to me in all your swimming strength of love for what must never be lost, and yet is lost—lake by lake.

Let the blood of my heart be as pure as water fresh from the fields of snow, you wrote in your Easter Sermon. I say, *You are here and Alive in me*. I hold out an oar. Just hold out your hand.

RUST NEEDS SOME SLEEP

Welcome to the Ivy League. Even Mr. Very Late Night finally succumbed.

Bob had passed out beneath a Navajo blanket on the kitchen table, his face buried in *The Origin of Consciousness in the Breakdown of the Bicameral Mind.* (I'll say this for the people I hung out with then, they passed out in front of interesting books.) Caitlin and I had whatever sex the thin raft of my single bed allowed. I don't know if Pete heard or not. The rule had always been if anybody got lucky, all the rules went out the window. I had the feeling that a lot of things were about to go out the window. The small-town school grapevine being what it was, everyone would know about Caitlin and me by noon at the very latest. Jim Briggs would probably know much sooner.

Caitlin didn't seem at all perturbed. She woke up blandly, kissed me and wandered out to make coffee, finding Bob pretzeled into a yoga shape. Not knowing a female was onboard, Bob almost tore a hamstring, especially since Caitlin was only wearing one of my T-shirts. I can't remember if anyone took any special interest in us that day. I was too excited and strung out to pay attention. Besides, Caitlin and I cut classes and took off on an adventure picnic, discovering a giant turkey farm and a lake covered in a little village of shacks where men were ice fishing.

Maybe that's why the news didn't upset me more. Or the fact that it was news to me. She wasn't living at Number 1 anymore, their name for their communal house. She'd left Jim a couple of weeks before. She'd moved in with Brian DeWit, who was renting a house in the neighboring village. But only temporarily. She and another girl named Andrea were going to rent a place across the river. Andy had already moved in.

But it got worse. Not only had she run off with Brian (of course "run off" was the last way she'd have described it—that was too old-fashioned and chauvinistic), she'd fucked him backwards and forwards and then decided he wasn't quite right. The funny thing is that he and Andy had hit it off. Well, sort of. It seems (and I wasn't to know this) that Brian and Andy were the perfect match (both snide, eat-the-wounded types)—but Brian was having trouble sexually. He hadn't had any trouble with *her*, Caitlin smiled, but apparently getting it up with Andy was a different matter (I don't know if the fact that her nickname was Andy was a factor or not).

That night we drove over to Brian DeWit's house to grab what few things she had there and then we went to the new place she was renting with Andy. Brian wasn't at his place; he was over talking critical theory with Andy. When they weren't saying things like, "For Derrida, the destruction of metaphysics means that every word becomes a found object," they were happily cutting each other's throats. You could tell that with a bit more alcohol their conversation would turn into something out of *No Exit* or *Who's Afraid of Virginia Woolf?* Brian offered me a Scotch and I accepted. When he offered me another I told him no thanks, I'd felt the click.

"The click!" he shouted. "Wait! I know that one. It's from a play. Tennessee Williams. *Cat on a Hot Tin Roof*, right?"

"Maybe I will have another one," I said. No wonder Brian was having trouble sticking it to Andy. He was so tightly wound I thought he might have a seizure. After dinner and a "debate" that erupted into a gender brawl (surprise!), Caitlin's mother telephoned to check if Caitlin had moved in, obviously a little concerned about the musical beds her daughter was playing. As the conversation appeared destined to last a while, and with Brian and Andy trucking off to see a Godard film, Caitlin chucked me the keys to her car and told me to go for a drive. After all, not having a car, I was probably "itching" to. I hated to admit it, but she was right. I'd sold my old bomb back in California to try to meet the costs the scholarship and the student loans didn't cover. I'd been hoofing it, hitching or busing ever since, and it felt fantastic to be vehicular again. If nothing else, I'd scored a babe with a car. But something about the situation reminded me of being in the student loan office with Mr. Quinty, signing another promissory note.

Naturally I had to assert my free will and God-given ability to screw things up by driving Caitlin's car onto the snowbound golf course. Maybe I was looking for Captain Galaxy. I almost rolled a couple of times and then I slid down an embankment. When I tried to power back up the rise, I lost traction and spun out onto a pond, which served as a very wicked water hazard between two fairways. Another baptism. I couldn't get any traction on the sheer ice, and a shuddering bubble sound gave me the fear.

I got out quickly. No one was around. The clouded surface of the pond hid a blue-black depth of reed and walleye. Gingerly I tried pushing the car but I slipped and fell. The pond ice trembled.

To make a long and embarrassing story short, I stood there for a while, wondering what in the hell to do and then realized that I only had one choice. I had to hike all the way to the old apartment and roust Bob and Pete to come help me—hoping to hell they'd both be home and that the car hadn't fallen through the ice by the time we got back. With their help I was able to roll the Honda safely off the pond. Of course I never told Caitlin what happened—or almost happened. I drove back to her place with my tail between my legs and we had a hot bath together and read some Yeats. Then we had sex.

We started having a lot of sex. At least I think it was sex. It seems now, in memory, more like the insatiable making of monsters—building them together then losing track of where the creatures slipped off. All they left behind were moisture stains and trails of slime, the scent of salt and fern. Somewhere in the midst of it all (about a week later) I moved in with her (at her suggestion, of course). From Bob and Pete's point of view I just up and left. I don't remember what I said but I remember Bob saying that I didn't have to say anything.

One night I went back to have dinner with Bob and Pete and settle the accounts. My sudden departure had upset the economics of their little world and, I was both pleased and saddened to realize, the emotional balance too. I found Bob chopping onions with his ski goggles on. He'd taken a break from his kabalistic studies to create a large multimedia art piece based on the Krebs cycle. For a moment I felt the old joy again, the warmth and energy of the collective intelligence. We were always on the verge of some immense breakthrough in those days. That was our binding certainty. "We're going off-road," Pete would say when a new line of questioning emerged. The answer could be hiding anywhere—in a Yaqui deer dance song or Boolean algebra. "You have to be ready to retool at a moment's notice," he proclaimed. "Jettison all assumptions—reconfigure the belief systems. The next secret you learn could be *the* Secret."

I may have realized that I would never know people like that again. Maybe that's why I felt so torn to be back eating with them. Bob had made Mexican-style spaghetti. It looked like a traffic accident but tasted great, a far cry from the Moroccan spiced calamari and fig tagine with mint and thyme-buttered couscous that Caitlin had introduced me to.

Already they'd tried to secure an alternate rent-payer but the experience had been a disaster. The guy had taken what he thought was some drug like Ecstasy (but which was probably PCP) and freaked out following a midnight showing of *Eraserhead*. He stayed awake all night playing the empty hangers in my closet with a butcher knife and then wandered outside in the morning stark naked singing "White Christmas." Shades of cousin Dennis (who never did become a cold-blooded killer, just a small-town historian and permanent bachelor-closeted gay with anger management issues).

"Remember," Bob said as I was leaving, "hyenas are matriarchal."

"Stay off the ice," Pete waved.

A week later I found myself back at the apartment again, staying over. It was in repayment for them helping me move the car off the ice. Bob and Pete had gone to Sugarbush to go skiing with these twin sisters from Holyoke, and my task was to babysit Bob's new puppy, Aquinas (who of course was totally outside the terms of the lease). I had a bag of dirty clothes and a hit of mescaline and I thought I'd swing by Koin-Kleen, do my laundry, have a bit of head time and repay the favor all at once. I made myself a burger and read for a couple of hours, played with the pup a while, took him outside and then stowed him in his box by Bob's bed, popped my mescaline and headed for the laundromat.

As the drug started taking effect, I began to feel waves of guilt and anxiety about Jim Briggs, Caitlin's ex. Why was I going to Koin-Kleen, which was *right* beside their old house—where Jim still lived? We're always playing tricks on ourselves, that was Freud's whole point, and making my way through the winter streets that night I started to see that I was walking into a snare I'd set for myself. I must've wanted to see Jim.

There was no one else in the laundromat. I could've just started the wash and gone in the other direction, but now I was consciously curious about the goings-on next door. The downstairs curtains were open and he was sitting in the living area. All the lights were out but he had a massive fire roaring. Through the window, I could see that he'd actually stoked the fireplace with the house's chopping block, complete with the hickory handled wood-splitting maul still embedded in it.

He had on Neil Young's *Rust Never Sleeps* and was plopped in his reading chair clutching a bottle of Jack Daniels. At his feet were scattered books and what looked like the shredded remains of his honors thesis, while strewn over the floor were the remnants of a Halloween party—miniature Snickers bars, string-pull skeletons and cheap plastic masks. Made me think of my sister . . . at the time lost to Christianity, urinary tract infections and New Jersey.

Every once in a while, Jim would take a slug of Jack and fumble down for another of the Halloween masks or a fistful of pages and toss them in the fire. One of the masks blew back out of the fire and fell smoldering on the floor. My brain festered with the mescaline—and then the burning witch's mask fluttered out of the flames and I thought—*Holy shit, the place is going to catch on fire.*

Knowing I had to act and yet knowing I was almost paralyzed, I thrust out my arm too hard and burst the fragile membrane between us. But it was only because I busted the windowpane that Jim heard me over the music. He turned, spilled his whiskey, rose from his chair and stumbled all in one motion, releasing a monstrous cyclone of shadows in the room. My hand was bleeding. Hypnotized by the sight of it, I held it up to what light there was coming from the Koin-Kleen sign. *Hey, hey,* Neil Young was singing.

"Fuck, man," Jim mumbled and I almost lost what slippery hold I had on the moment because he had a set of those glow-in-the-dark green fangs in his mouth. Then I shot past him and began stamping wildly on the floor, where the mask had set fire to a section of throw rug. As liquid as the room appeared, I could tell Jim was too drunk to have known about the fire. Even the fumes didn't seem to worry him. The fat-boy woodstove was empty and cold—all the available wood had been piled into the fireplace, heat soaring up the chimney.

"Wan beer?" he hollered over the music, gumming the phosphorescent wax fangs out of his mouth and flinging them into the fireplace. The visual information was becoming too intense for me to process. I had to sit down, and thankfully, I found a stained old hassock, like an older version of the one I had climbed on top of to peer inside Alicia Sandringham's cuckoo clock.

Jim had what looked like the remains of several day-old Hawaiian pizzas spread out on the kitchen table and the floor—one slice stuck to the bottom of his waffle-stomper hiking boot. Swigging Black Jack and gnawing at a hunk of dough, he kicked his way through the debris on the floor and collapsed back into his chair. Then he squeezed the bottle between his knees and rummaged beneath the chair, producing a large green rubber mask of Yoda from *Star Wars*. He crammed the rest of the pizza into his mouth and then wrenched the mask over his skull.

"There was a fire!" I yelled over Neil Young.

"There's the fire," Yoda answered, pointing to the red molten mountain. "Wanna shot?"

I intended to decline the whiskey but I needed something to cut the hallucinations. Although mescaline is more of a surface drug than acid or mushrooms, the colors and the mood were overloading my brain. I kept turning around to see what I was missing out of the corner of my eye and then I'd find Yoda trying to drink Jack Daniels and debating whether or not to sacrifice *The Portable Nietzsche*.

"I have . . . to go," I said. Or tried to say. Maybe I just thought it. Something about laundry—and screwing up Jim's wife. His life.

How long I sat there I can't be sure. The shadows changed so the fire must've burned down. The music was long over. In fact another album had come on. The Clash? I couldn't remember what we'd listened to. Time had just been sucked out of the room like the heat up the chimney. Jim was gone too. There was just Yoda, trampled Snickers bars and shreds of Nietzsche.

"I have to go," I said.

How many times had I said that? I remembered my laundry. I was worried that it would freeze in the washing machine. Why would it freeze? Maybe I should throw it all onto the fire. Save me the cost of the dryer. Maybe I was only imagining that I had a load of laundry next door. What about the pup?

"I have to go," I said.

"The worsht enemy yoo can-encounner will always be yoo, yersself. Yoo lie in wait for yersself in caves an' woods," Yoda quoted.

Shit, I thought. No wonder I'm paranoid.

The voice spoke again. It was Jim's voice. Behind the green latex-smelling face, I thought he'd blacked out. But he stirred and took another slurp.

Finally I managed to say. "I'm sorry, Jim. About Caitlin."

An immense labor to talk. I noticed that he'd dragged himself out of his chair and baited what looked like a very large and malicious rat trap beside the refrigerator with a piece of the Hawaiian pizza. He could barely walk but he managed to arm the spring-jawed device without snapping a finger off.

"Be of good chair, Luke Skywalker," he giggled and then made a sound like he was vomiting inside the mask, but he was only hawking up some phlegm. He grabbed a long-necked beer out of the fridge, lit another Camel and returned to his chair. The fire burned down. He threw some pieces of chopped-up stool on. The embers gleamed up into flames. I drank another beer. He told me he was actually glad she was gone—that it was over. Then he started crying.

It was a dreadful sound, coming from inside the Yoda mask. Gus Gus revisited. Then when I realized he was sobbing his guts out, I wanted to put my arm around his shoulder. But it seemed so pathetic. Of course I felt a sharp wire of guilt prodding me. I'd benefited from his misery. Or so I thought at the time. More fool me.

The sun was coming up. It looked like one of those remorseful alcoholic mornings. A day of frost-coated branches and treacherous black-ice sidewalks.

Jim yanked the Yoda mask over his head and flung it into the kitchen. It struck the rat trap when it hit the floor and the steel spring almost barked, it sounded so loud. Like one of my father's burps. Jim paid no attention. His eyes were bleary with rheum and tears but his voice was sober now—that creepy lock-up-the-knives sober you get to when you've been on the hooch or crank too long.

"Wan some breakfast?" he asked, opening another beer.

"I have to go," I said. This time I kept my promise.

I started walking home down the slick, dark street, examining the dried blood on my hand. Then I remembered my laundry. When I got back to Koin-Kleen I could hear that Jim had on some band I'd never heard before at peak volume. It was so loud it vibrated out of the mouths of the empty washing machines. As quick as I could, I shoved my damp clothes into a dryer, fed it with change and headed back to check on the pup. I didn't want to be in there when the cops arrived to get him to turn down the stereo.

POWDER MONKEYS

Frank's furtive, simian behavior certainly did concern me, but I was keeping close tabs on him with my hand on the trigger of a dry-chem fire extinguisher. He was actually starting to appear vaguely crustacean.

Meanwhile, I seemed to have lost control of my forehead. It kept furrowing and unfurrowing. Two weeks of pure methedrine had taken its toll on both of us, and his girlfriend seemed headed for the loony bin (but we were philosophical about this, because she'd seemed like an excellent candidate for that from the start).

I was on the verge of either laughing hysterically or weeping at virtually *anything* I thought of (including the panic of not having a clear thought to mumble), while Frank was obsessed with an old Dinah Washington song on a record he'd found in a junk shop, called "I Sold My Heart to the Junk Man." He played it continuously, and I mean continuously, because he was afraid that if he didn't, the world would end. (I was somewhat sympathetic to this reasoning, having only a month before been similarly fixated on the Steely Dan song "Babylon Sisters.")

Outside it was snowing softly, and the flakes looked like .17 Remington shots colliding with raindrops.

I don't know how I managed to pry him out of that room and away from that damn record. He'd become convinced his heart would stop beating if the needle slipped off that one song—and given the amount of crank we'd snorted, the Vegas money might've backed him.

We were in that paralysis mode of the wire—just after a hyperspeed light trail Ping-Pong duel down in the basement of the dormitory, where it was warm from the oil heater, so we'd both broken out in a blood sweat and had worked off the first edge of the rush. Muscles had started contracting since then, and the desire for movement wasn't connecting with the nerves to make that comfortably possible.

Once we got out into the cold, though, I knew we'd start throwing snowballs and darting around like fools behind the trees, dilated eyes wide for narcotics agents and those creepy shadow men who are only as thick as plate glass that you often catch sight of on a speed freak. I thought it was worth the risk.

We stood under the halo of an antique-looking streetlamp in the falling snow for about two hundred years. I was bawling my eyes out about dead family and friends—and how hot Frank's sister looked when she wore that fluorescent green leotard. Frank had his head thrown back, catching dirty snowflakes on his tongue and snickering like some demented crab lord—his afro silver with snow crystals like a luminous dandelion.

Earlier, he'd planted an idea related to eating—something we hadn't been doing a lot of lately, but which was now moving up on our priority list. Unfortunately, he'd introduced the topic in the context of a pineapple ham steak at the Village Green, which struck me as the most ridiculous idea I'd ever heard of (knowing that the place had been closed for more than four hours), and set me laughing so hard I might've burst a vein had he not zinged me with an iceball that hit me in the forehead (that was still wrinkling and unwrinkling of its own accord) with such force I thought the streetlamp had exploded.

This prompted a recommendation on my part that we borrow the car of a guy we called The Big-Mouth Bass for a high-speed run down to Manchester and Dunkin' Donuts. We knew for a fact the Bass was blacked out from a keg party and wouldn't miss his keys until noon the next day. We, on the other webbed hand, still had another gram. Having almost knocked me cold with the overly compressed snowball (Frank was, after all, a former all-city pitcher in high school and had been scouted by the pros), he could hardly refuse.

I think I handled the swerve on the interstate to avoid the deer with great finesse and that highly tuned amphetamine alertness we both so enjoyed. I also brought my diplomatic skills to bear in Dunkin' Donuts when Frank collapsed in an unsightly cackling fit at the word *cruller* (which he made sound like it had five syllables). And I humored his craving for a pineapple and ham pizza (which was not easy to come by at 3 AM) to complement his toffee cream butter-horn for the drive back.

What I'm particularly proud of to this day is my deft, determined crossing of the snowbound, grassy median when I realized I'd somehow gotten on the wrong side of the interstate (the backs of the signs was my clue). I thought that not to have gotten us hopelessly bogged or skidded out of control was a fine effort on my part, but all Frank could say was, "You want a peeth of piztha?"

So it is with friends. They get used to us, and take our shining moments for granted. A moment later he asked, "Do you know why the sun's rising?"

I thought of the cosmology class I was nearly failing for lack of attendance. "I have a general idea," I said.

"It's because I left the record on," he said proudly. "I jammed the needle. It's been going the whole damn time we've been gone!"

Aha, I thought. So it is with friends. We get used to them, and take their shining moments for granted.

SENTENCED TO DISNEYLAND

Here you leave today and enter the world of yesterday, tomorrow and fantasy—the magical portals to the Magic Kingdom.

"This was the American dream, a prayer for the future. But that golden goal was not to be had without cost. The American Way was not gained in a day. It was born in adversity, forged out of conflict."

Conflict?

Let me tell you about conflict. It's watching two of the Seven Dwarves kick the shit out of each other in costume in one of the backstage areas and hearing one rant, "You gave me herpes!"

Conflict is on one of your days off thinking it would be very funny to drop a hit of acid with your craziest friend and toodle around the park as if you were a civilian . . . only to find yourself peaking on the "It's a Small World" ride, which gets stuck, while the song keeps playing over and over, the animatronic dolls representing all the cultures of the world squeaking, "It's a small world after all, it's a small world after all . . . " while the world does indeed get smaller as the drug comes on harder, a pregnant claustrophobic woman begins to sob, children become dangerously excited—and your lunatic friend rises and begins singing the song at the top of his voice.

We were very fortunate not to have been taken away in a net on that one—and when you get expelled from the Magic Kingdom, before you find yourself in lockup in downtown Anaheim, you get a special debriefing by park security behind closed doors, a prospect that was considerably more hallucinogenic than I could cope with.

Remarkably, we escaped the small world, and beyond a minor incident on Mr. Toad's Wild Ride (where I found it necessary to physically restrain my friend Steve), I was able to return to my normal duties two days later, although *normal* was always a relative term.

I worked as a "cast member" captaining the *Amazon Belle* on the Jungle Cruise in Adventureland . . . and here verbatim is the spiel (which we were taught to refer to as "the preset narrative") that I'd recite. After you've delivered this little speech three times, you begin to get the disturbing impression that you've been turned into an animatronic character yourself.

> Here we go deep into a tropical rainforest. Yeah, it rains 365 days a year here. Over on the other side there's old Smiley, one of my favorite jungle residents—and also one of the craziest crocs in these parts, folks. Nobody's seen him move for over thirty years. What a croc!
>
> And that there is a Bengal tiger, folks. He weighs over five hundred pounds and can jump up to twenty-five feet from a dead standstill. Oh, look at this, the little headhunters! Watch out, folks! And beautiful Schweitzer Falls. Named after that famous African explorer, Dr. Albert Falls. Uh-oh, a huge African bull elephant. For those of you with short memories, that there is a huge African bull elephant.
>
> Hang on now. Hippos! Got to scare them off. Cover your ears. We're back in headhunter country now. Not a good place to be headed. Those are spears—and those are poison arrows.

> If any of them hit you folks, you throw them right on back—you're not allowed to keep any souvenirs. Now let me take this opportunity to point out some of the rare tropical foliage to you. There's some. And there's some more over there.
>
> And there's old Trader Sam, the head trader for the area, folks, but business has been shrinking a little lately. He's got a special deal going—two of his heads for just one of yours. And folks, you don't wanna miss this. This might be your only opportunity to see a rare African mallard. Oh, what do you know, we're returning to civilization. This could well be the most dangerous part of our journey. You have to careful. Not all the animals are in the jungle. Ha-ha.

Yes, this was the American dream, a prayer for the future. Where the Matterhorn rises over Frontierland next to the Enchanted Tiki Village. Now a thrilling adventure cruise through dark, mysterious caverns where dead men tell no tales. Clear the decks, lad! Remember, the American Way was not gained in a day. It was born in adversity and forged out of conflict. Strike your colors, you bloomin' cockroaches! By thunder!

(That bit about the mallard was my improv, by the way. You couldn't always count on the ducks being in position to have them written into the script. Funny about that.)

HEAR THE WIND BLOW, DEAR

Back—to the summer nights sweltering with chocolate from the Peter Paul factory—back to the stinking aurora of the sugar refinery poised at the railhead beyond the black field of beets.

My friends and I drove drunk to the top of Mount Toro in full moonlight. We were gulping Guinness Stout, which was hard to come by then, and I was in love—with the warm air on my bare chest, with cigarettes, and the rich foam, with some seventeen-year-old girl whose name I don't even remember—and we staggered to nostalgic rock 'n' roll under the giant television tower that dominates the peak.

We gazed out over the luminous irrigation canals that artery the land where Steinbeck set his novels of ice and lettuce and imaginary rabbit necks broken by big hands.

Far across the valley, the lights of a long tanker truck crept south down the interstate. I cracked another beer and stared at the moon, my nerves tingling into kindling—into cattails—into particles of light beamed from a satellite.

Suddenly, I began to rise, leaving my friends straggling and kissing on the dry grass below. I wanted to holler down—*Hey, look at me, the Man Drinking Beer in the Moon*. But my eyes were drawn to a dark gully that lay beyond their field of vision.

The hull of an old Chevrolet and the stripped chassis of some other anonymous car lounged in the cleft where only the moonlight could find them. They might've belonged to our parents—kids of an earlier generation who came, like us, to the top of the mountain, to neck, pet, spoon, spark—whatever people under the influence of adolescence feel compelled to do. Maybe the drivers of those cars never returned. Maybe they're still here, I thought.

I saw the girl I was with, down below. She was sneaking off to take a leak, her big white breasts puffing the gauze of her shirt. I saw her father's merchant marine hands delicately spinning a screwdriver in the back of a TV repair shop. I saw her father and mother kissing in the front seat of a hot rod.

Sweethearts have always come here, I realized. Now their children born of bourbon and a slow dance flee the air-conditioned houses to follow their young ghosts—but we can't drink with them or dance or watch new satellites creep across the sky. We're too grown up to know we're all here together. Soon a new generation will come to look for us just when they're trying to escape. And I sank back down to join those of my age.

But if I had known that night what I would one day lose, I would've listened more intently to my old young friends. I would've kept a closer watch on the lights of that tanker as we swallowed the thick stout that night. And I would've given up the dream of rising above the skeletal transmitter and the abandoned Chevrolets of love.

Faith. That was the girl who wandered off. Faith Harding.

ONE LONG WHISTLE

We could hear a train coming long before we'd see it, so there was almost always plenty of time to tightrope on the trestle rails—to tense the watch-springs in our legs and leap into thirty-five feet of pure July—because nothing sounds as beautiful as a freight train heard underwater.

At first we were scared to dive down with a mask. There were headless corpses decomposing in the mud—better vague shapes seen through blurred eyes. But the mystery of what was *really* down there beckoned. So, one by one we spat in Michael's scuba glass, pretending we were frogmen mining the bridge.

We found a cash register, filled with snail shells, that came from a robbery at the Liquor Mart. We found the obligatory bottles and shoes. But beyond even our secret expectations—we found a Pontiac parked permanently like a Matchbox car in a murky aquarium.

Here was a heaven for escape artists and archaeologists—to fill our lungs with sunlight and wriggle through the eel grass, *to swim through the splintered windshield and slip alone behind the wheel.*

We even found a doll trapped beneath a seat. Half tadpole, half Chatty Cathy—each of us attempted the rescue—slithering up a rope of bubbles to break the surface with the body of the baby clutched in one hand. It became a game of hiding and seeking and saving. But we always returned her, so that she would be there waiting.

On my last birthday, I returned to that town for the first time in a million years and found Michael married to a pretty girl who was getting fat. We drank a case of Pabst Blue Ribbon. Then some obese truck driver with a Rip Van Winkle beard showed up with a couple of kilos of Mexican gold he'd smuggled back in a shipment of birdseed.

We cleaned some and rolled it, and eventually smoked it. Then we sat back in an afternoon stupor and talked inevitably of the old days. We covered the important subjects like drunk driving and sex in cemeteries. We spoke of jobs we hated, dead parents, kids, computer games and the downward trend in the quality of cartoons.

Suddenly, Michael's eyes glazed over with what looked like an idea, and he disappeared—only to burst back in the room with a big eureka grin on his face.

Very slowly from behind his back, he revealed the doll I thought we'd decided not to save. She'd been cleaned up, but there was no mistaking who or what it was. He looked at me as if to say, "Remember?" and I just smiled.

I couldn't explain how disappointed I was. Seeing the doll should've meant something, but as soon as I did, I realized she should've remained in the drowned car. She didn't belong in a bungalow—she belonged down with the catfish and the empty Fanta cans.

And if she'd managed to survive on the surface, the believer in me expected her to have grown into a pretty girl with a new car—maybe even children of her own. It was time for me to leave.

Rip was eyeing Beth's big tits and Michael was on the nod. But he staggered out to the car with me, and as I sat behind the wheel in the dry early September air, I asked him, "Do you remember what that sign said at the end of the trestle? You know, the big yellow sign we passed every time? The instruction for the engineer?"

He thought about it—scratched his chin, smiled sadly and said, "Naw."

I'd been gunning the engine, and when I pressed the accelerator to the floor, I took one last look and saw him still wondering—and wondering what I meant.

So I pushed my hand down on the horn and held it there, green willows weeping slowly gold in both mirrors when I crossed the bridge.

THE GULF OF CALIFORNIA

You know what I miss most, Anna? Watching you try to fold maps. And the way you always waited until you were in the car to spray on your perfume.

Do you still drive out through the oil derricks when you need time to think? Can you still drive? My father says he can, and he's been dead as long as you.

I miss the smell of your skin when you got hot dancing—sitting in those cane chairs, listening to that stupid parrot of your aunt's.

My old man comes back at night to drink Old Crow with me. Old man, old crow. He knows. Why did I ever pity him?

Come back and smell like limes and White Shoulder perfume and we'll drink Tanqueray and ice. Come back to me and we'll count mirages all the way to Enseñada. Please.

I have one arm out the window—and one hand on the wheel. I'm about to cross the border in a haunted car, with two arrests and no convictions. Someone to declare.

ALLIGATOR WISHES

If for no other reason, I'm proud to live on a planet that was once ruled by reptiles.

You can call my pilgrimage a tribute to those ancestral origins or just a private crisis, but I had to return to the scene of our foggy morning field trips—to the smell of peanut-butter-and-banana sandwiches and the echo of speakers explaining luminous sponges.

For some, the highlight of the Steinhart Aquarium—next door to the Tea Garden and the de Young Museum—was the dolphin tank. For me, the essence was the slick stone pit that would've made an evil Oriental genius envious.

Below lurked the supreme monsters—serene in their scales, with yellow eyes, teeth and tails for thrashing. Many were the discussions held against the iron fence about what would happen should one of us fall amongst those distant relatives. They seemed so sleepy and aloof. What would it be like when the slippery rocks suddenly came alive?

Like all children, we thought we were the first to ever gaze down on the jaws and armor in the moat. Yet even a casual glance revealed this wasn't the case.

Other children on other field trips had made of the pit, a wishing well. Pennies, nickels, dimes, even one silver dollar glistened in the water, and if you looked through the opera glasses that Jenny Lehman, the smartest girl in our class, had snitched from her mother—you could at least think you saw coins embedded in the umber leather of what we reckoned was the oldest lizard of them all.

We were not ones to break with tradition. When the guards and teachers weren't watching, we surreptitiously splashed our coins and made our wishes, wondering if when we were grown, our children wouldn't one day find an alligator adorned with a piece of a field trip, lost forever for safekeeping.

That's what I went back to see. Foolishly, I thought I could spy the coin I dropped fifteen years before as easily as I remembered the wish I'd made. Innocence, innocence. No sense.

I found instead a sign clearly posted that said: DO NOT THROW COINS . . . THEY CAN DAMAGE THE HEALTH OF THE ANIMALS. THANK YOU.

So much for innocence. I made a wish without throwing a coin for Jenny Lehman.

I left the dark, watery calm of the aquarium thinking there is perhaps a place, a pool—where if we cared or dared to, we could find the reflections of our younger faces—and if we stared through a pair of opera glasses, maybe we could count the gleaming eyes of all our wishes that never came true, yet still survive and give us hope, poisonous though they may have been.

LETTERS FROM OLD GIRLFRIENDS

Consider this letter from a Marina Del Rey girl named Meg, written on stationery from the Reef Hotel on Waikiki Beach.

I must tell you what happened Thursday before I left. I was out walking in the residential part of Beverly Hills, going to a friend's house, when this bird flew really close, then it flew back and attacked my back—then my head! I almost dropped dead on the street from fright! I hit it into a tree with my sweater and ran down the street screaming. All the Mexican gardeners just looked at me like I was insane!

How many girls write boys about their bird attacks?

Meg and I fooled around one summer. This was way back in high school. I'm talking way back. She lived with her father, who was in show business and very rich. Her mother was in rehab and then moved to Maui, where Meg went to join her. The strange thing is that I had a pair of her panties hanging on the curtain rod over my bed. I'm not sure how I got them. My mother never said a word. One day another girlfriend noticed them and asked me about them. Did I ever try them on? (I took them down after that.) She remarked that they were very expensive.

What was I thinking? Why did I have them hanging over my

bed? Was I trying to imply that I'd banged Meg? Had I banged Meg? Maybe. It was hard to remember exactly what happened that summer.

I certainly could've banged Meg, judging from the pile of letters she wrote me, all of them signed *Love Ya, Babe* or *Aloha foxy. Stay high and save some for me.*

She had a killer body. Her face was a bit witchy, but knowing what I know now, she was just the kind of girl who would've turned into a ripsnorter of a honey. And she really cared for me. I think. *Every time I look at your picture I sit down and cry. I just came home from Marie Callender's Pies, where I ate so much I feel like I'm going to throw up.*

There may have been an eating disorder at work, not to mention a lot of hash smoking, but she knew Warren Beatty (*he doesn't look anything like himself*) and she got backstage passes to concerts.

There are hundreds of other letters I saved, which is suspicious. Did I need to prove to myself that I existed and was desired—that girls wrote to me? Some are scratched in a cramped, careless hand. Others, meticulous and marshaled, character by character. Still others are dreamy and swirly, full of smiling faces and flower sketches. Such earnestness and emotion.

A girl named Ellen told me some about the secret "lights" we have to give away. *Most people don't give their lights away for the simple fact that they don't know they have them! I mean, they know that they have love to give away, but not this special love, this secret and beautiful person love!*

Another girl, Audrey, wrote a letter to me on her forget-me-not personal letterhead in her Great Books class. It's a tease letter. And a damn good one at that. All these years later, you can still see her, line by curvy flowery line, getting off, putting down on her creamy personal letterhead thoughts she shouldn't have been having, at least not in an Advanced Placement class. She could be dead of breast cancer now, for all I know. And yet decades and dead marriages later I'm holding this forget-me-not, vaguely perfume-scented letter that looks like it could've been written yesterday.

Then there's this one from Marti—still smelling of muskmelon and Cuervo Gold.

I don't want you to think of me as a fickle bitch that can't make up her mind. If you'll remember I told you first I loved you. I meant it and I still do. I will always love you. I just wish I met you a little later, when I get my shit together.

Ah me. A brush-off letter. From a girl who tasted like a tequila shooter and whose brother made cherry bombs in the sad heavy metal of his little valley room.

I can't bring myself to throw the note away even now—with its silhouettes of two lovers on a beach and all the tender, honest mindless talk of *hurt* and *missing you already*. I particularly find it hard not to laugh when I think about the waves breaking behind the lovers, because in a hot and sweaty moment of teen lust, I once reclined the seat of my mother's silver Toyota Corona (what a choice for romance), pulled down the girlfriend's jeans and went down on her in the little parking area of Point Lobos. Things were getting very wet and squirmy indeed, when I chanced to glance up and realized that a large Golden California tour bus had pulled in right beside us, filled with wide-eyed senior citizens all glued to the window in shock.

And then there is the missive that the infamous Kane McNally sent me.

I am well aware of the fact that I blew it between us last night. I've realized 2 things because of this. 1.) Until you hurt someone you love you don't realize just how much you cared. The 2nd is that when something is valuable to you, once you've lost it, you find out just how much it meant. Please, please tell me how you feel. Believe me I need to know. With much of my love, Kane.

Well, Kane, I haven't yet made up my mind how I feel. (The fact that you later coaxed the gang of Thai boxers into trying to kick my ribs in at Shakey's Pizza may have something to do with it.) But I'm honestly still trying to cope with that two-part epiphany of yours. Was that one realization or two? And as to my *respect and understanding* that apparently meant so much, what about the moraine-blue glitter in your eyes and that fine ass, as smooth and round as a clove of garlic? That's what I was interested in. I wanted to smell your hair and ride the roller coaster in Santa Cruz with you. Peel off that stonewashed denim and explore the tide pool with a thick length of kelp.

Years later I saw Kane weaving out of a cheap motel room at the bottom of University Avenue in Berkeley, her eyes vacant with smack. Somehow I don't think the man she'd been with had showed her much respect and understanding. I couldn't even gloat. *Even if it were possible that you still cared I would probably just hurt you again.*

Right you are, Kane. On a still, gray day, a lifetime later, you *can* still make me sad again, even though I suspect you're now beyond all hurt yourself.

SEX AND DEATH

A bleak, grim, Boeing day, a slow mist falling like reminder notices for overdue books, and there it is, in the mailroom of Padelford Hall, home of the University of Washington's English department . . . Scotch-taped to the pigeonholes, in simple black felt pen: DOES ANYONE HAVE AN ELECTRIC RAZOR FOR RICHARD HUGO?

It shocks me, because the Richard Hugo in question is a famous American poet, judge of the Yale Younger Poets series and author of a whole shelf of neat books. I leave without checking my mail.

Hugo is back home in Seattle, having lived in Montana, Iowa and the Isle of Skye, and he's dying of leukemia. From his hospital bed, perhaps he can look out over the battlements of I-5 and see the ferries to Bainbridge and Vashon Islands, the red cranes and derricks in the shipping yards—or on the other side of the city, traffic strung out over the Evergreen Point Floating Bridge. I don't even know what hospital he's in. Harborview Medical Center? Does it matter? He just needs a shave.

He's a local boy originally, from White Center/West Seattle—a former student of Theodore Roethke at the university, like James Wright. (I remember feeling so proud that my first poems published in *The Hudson Review* appeared alongside some of Wright's last.) Roethke's reputation still lingers around the campus, even though morale in the English department is appalling. The glory days are gone.

That Richard Hugo would be dying doesn't surprise me. What bothers me is that pathetic plea for an electric razor. Wouldn't an awarding-winning man, a writer of his standing, have an electric razor? Couldn't someone buy one for him? I wondered . . . should I buy one for him? Should I go down to Nordstrom's and buy a brand new Norelco electric for Richard Hugo? Shiny stainless steel with three floating heads?

What about his family? His friends? And then I think that we in the English department are his friends, his family. But how can that be? He's never given a reading in my time there. Never visited a class or wandered the halls, that I know of. Perhaps he's a prick, leukemia or not. A boozy technical writer of a trout fisherman who just learned how to con Eastern academics, with images of derelict mining town taverns full of ruptured old-timers and abandoned women who smell of dirty diapers.

And how am I *in* the English department anyway? I'm only a graduate student teaching rhetoric to pay my way. Why should I feel guilty about Richard Hugo? Just because I was given his best book, *What Thou Lovest Well Remains American*, for one of the awards I won back in college—and read every word as slowly as I'd sip hot soup?

I couldn't understand it then, the gray Seattle sadness of autumn colors running in the rain, and the fact that people die every day, yet the phone bills still arrive. The fact that steaks are still ordered with sautéed mushrooms and none of us can ever really care much about anything beyond our own comfort or suffering—not because we don't want to, but because we can't physically forgive ourselves for the selfishness we need to breathe, to fire a synapse, or to use our stereoscopic vision and opposable thumbs to raise our glasses in friendship. It's not in our power to be so free and so dependent on each other. Except in moments of dangerous lucidity.

If we could but see ourselves—published, awarded, even quietly famous, and still dying a dreadful death in a medium-size city full of gulls and rain, without the simple dignity of a proper supply of toiletries—we'd at least feel the need to read more poetry—or maybe to live more poetically. We'd rush onto a ferry and ride all the way to Bremerton just to watch a cloud of steam rise out of a sawmill, bald eagles unraveling the sky. We'd fling our musk and yearning at a young lover and get ourselves into all sorts of trouble, which we do anyway. And we still might die, lonely, undignified, emaciated, and begging for morphine—but we would've lived a little more.

On the other hand, maybe we wouldn't have the heart to get up out of our chairs. We'd just sit there, catatonic before the lobster tank. In any case, it's way too late for Richard Hugo. He died a short time after I broke one of my stiff standing rules and started fooling around with one of my students, an African goddess—not in some net-shrouded four-poster bed by the light of a hurricane lamp, but in the front seat of my then girlfriend's-and-later-another-wife's VW Rabbit, in the huge, anonymous parking lot below the campus, often with the rain thundering down on us like lug nuts and bicycle chains, breath clouding the windows (once, her big ass pushed one of my Spanish-language cassettes into the tape recorder when I had the ignition on to run the heater, and while she straddled me, we kept hearing in perfect rhythm, "Por favor! Por favor!").

Now I'm sad about Dick Hugo. I think of lines of his, like, "When you leave here, leave in a flashy car and wave goodbye. You are a stranger every day." Why couldn't the hospital staff shave him? When I was an orderly, I shaved men. True, it was usually their pubic hair in preparation for surgery, but the point is there were plenty of electric razors around. "You can prune the shrubbery, but leave the standing timber," one man tried to joke. He was a glum school principal, with a flaccid bratwurst lying sullenly between his legs.

I'm fairly certain Richard Hugo didn't have his crotch shaved. It wouldn't have done any good for his condition. And it wouldn't have been fair, seeing that no one would shave his face. A famous poet—and how many of those are there? That's what got me. That's what's taken all these years to process. Sure, every once in a while there's a presidential inauguration and they trot out some vintage champion of the sanctioned word—but outside these dismal ceremonial occasions and the flea market realm of the popular song, poetry has become a sanitized, museumized, dwindling folk art. Not the language of magic, the genesis code of all human striving. A neutered cliché.

I couldn't accept that then. In those days, I believed that Walt Whitman spoke to me personally through a battered Sony Walkman. I believed God or the Devil might very well be a brunette who wore red leather Florentine boots in bed and squealed in foul-mouthed conniption when I did her from behind. She had a husky, naughty-sorority-sister laugh and absolutely no idea what to do with herself; I can smell her pussy and her avocado shampoo even now.

Back then, I believed that everyone, from the Iranian waiter at Broadway Joe's to the Laotian gardeners beavering around the mansions of Lake Washington, was as impressed as I was by Dylan Thomas's grave in Westminster Abbey, with the concluding lines from "Fern Hill" laid into the floor: "Time held me green and dying, though I sang in my chains like the sea."

Something in me felt certain that this was more fundamental to our sense of society than sewage management, electricity, antibiotics, frozen vegetables or birth control.

I'm not saying we should've given Richard Hugo a parade. I don't even know how good a poet he was, really—how important he is now that poetry is about as culturally significant as pottery. The truth is I can't think about him at all without thinking about those lost days of my own in Seattle. The city where Thomas Wolfe died. Where Jimi Hendrix and Bruce Lee are buried.

I see the windows of the Swedish Hospital shining in the late afternoon light. A seaplane landing on Lake Union. Skid row ghosts of old loggers and longshoremen wandering somnolently across Pioneer Square. And me going bowling every morning in the basement of the Hub, the student union building, before teaching my composition class. "Zen bowling" I called it, as I wrapped a blindfold around my head (in a nod to my father's early swimming lessons), swigging espresso and giggling like a maniac.

Once, I taught a class in the same room where Roethke had held court—the same room where Richard Hugo and James Wright had sat taking notes. I was so excited my first day, I got to class early and then had to sit on a bench, smoking. I said to myself, "This is an important day. This day will set the tone. I will see visions and signs."

Then I looked down on the grass and there was this squirrel. Like the mythic squirrel that could cross whole sections of America jumping from tree to tree, just as I'd wanted to leap from roof to roof. But something was wrong with it. I got so curious I had to get up to take a closer look. I couldn't believe it. The squirrel, it seems, had found one of those little plastic buckets of tartar sauce they sell in the Hub, and had stuck its head in to eat the remains and gotten the tub firmly stuck on its head. It tried clawing the thing off. It tried rolling on the grass. It was hilarious. It was tragic. It was hypnotic. I couldn't decide whether to help or not. After all, squirrels do carry bubonic plague. (I was once attacked by a squirrel in Battery Park in New York, and that thought was much on my mind at the time.) Then I glanced around and realized that my interest in the situation had drawn a small crowd. People were starting to think that I'd done something to the squirrel, so I fled to class—the same room where Roethke had first read his poem "The Meadow Mouse."

All the other courses I taught were in the Mechanical Engineering building. Why English would be taught in the Mechanical Engineering building I have no idea. It was just another of those surreal disjunctions that I perversely savored. To highlight it, I made sure that if there were any equations on the blackboard, I always left them there, writing my notes and bullet points around them. It amused me that students would have to confront this collage of mathematical symbols and literary definitions.

I don't know what my students made of this—and I honestly didn't care. What I was trying to cope with were all the hot girls, of which I had many in my classes, and not that much younger in the big scheme of things. (The big scheme!)

It was all I could do to keep my door open during office hours. Many of the babes were literally bursting out of their blouses—glossy lipsticked, big-haired frat-row bombshells hoping for a B, and arty Goths with garage sale hats and black widow's gloves—all of them with asses as smooth and curving as Edward Weston's bell peppers.

I had lovely Chinese, Vietnamese, Cambodians, Nicaraguans, Samoans, Alaskans, and a whole lot of round, fleshy white girls with straight hair. These latter were mostly locals. They came from Enumclaw and Puyallup, Issaquah, Wenatchee, Toppenish, Cle Elum and Snoqualmie. They wore cottontail underwear, chewed sugarless gum, and took showers twice a day. They didn't care much about English, really. They cared about not throwing up at parties. They cared about their weight and their wardrobe. They cared about not getting pregnant and one day finding a good job—or at least a job. Many I suspect had toy animals in their rooms. Most stared surreptitiously at my crotch when I lectured, and all could be made to blush and giggle like flicking on a switch.

I had a hook-nosed Persian princess with a 40D cup giving me flowers and books, and a freckle-breasted hourglass redhead from Moses Lake writing me the most ungrammatical and touching love letters. I'd sometimes masturbate over them and burst into laughter and tears all at once. It was terribly flattering and exhilarating, and my manic passion for them drove me deep into my peers in the graduate program. Torrie, a raving feminist with trick legs and a mood disorder. Jacqueline, who wrote sad/funny stories she'd read to me over souvlaki and beer in Gas Works Park—forever debating whether she should go back to her deadbeat boyfriend in Olympia—and then banging me breathless in her studio apartment in Wallingford, filled with books by Willa Cather and Erica Jong.

I had a one-night stand with a witch who lived in Underground Seattle. She lived on salmon heads and fresh testicles she'd wok-fry in scalding sesame oil. And who could forget sweet Jane? Gifted with the firmest, shapeliest breasts I've ever fondled, but a complete and utter loon, who later tried to commit suicide, knowing that I was coming over—and so I had to break down her door in Ravenna and drive her to the University Hospital emergency room to get her stomach pumped.

There were countless other little frolics. Barely remembered gropes and pokes at parties. Pulling the wings off nurses. Holding hands in Queen Anne. Anal sex in Ballard (there's a title for you). Midnight drives down Aurora Avenue, with its ghoulish cocktail lounges and repossessed appliances, gun shops, car lots, and hotbox motels. Who can remember it all? Blow jobs. Bergman films. Big plans. I sank dick into pussy like burying fish to grow corn, as my Nez Perce friend Trey would say. I could ejaculate phosphorescent jellyfish in those days. Milky-wet sturgeon thrashing on the floor. I was so distraught by the loss of love from the woman I lived with, I did anything I could to get back at her—but even at my most insane, I could never keep up with her betrayals.

The real estate agent who was handling the mansion the demon girlfriend and I were caretaking once caught me sunbathing naked on the sprawling back lawn, reading a book. She was the bitchiest agent of them all, too—a flabby Cadillac arrest widow former prom queen turned lush, and there I was lying on the grass with a hard-on when she showed up unannounced. She looked down on it with an expression of pure disgust, then she hiked up her dress, whipped off her panties and sat down on it as if the world was coming to an end. Not one intelligible word. A fifty-five-year-old woman clawing me so that I had to wear a heavy T-shirt to bed for almost two weeks to hide the marks. She got so wet it was like trying to paddle a kayak up a waterfall. I never saw her again except in dreams.

Just as I never saw the Norwegian plasterer again. I had to call him after a pipe burst in one of the guest bathrooms. He would've been about thirty-five, but he had a Nordic baby face that made him look much younger. I was sun-baking out on the roof, reading *The Odyssey*, covered in Johnson's Baby Oil, when he appeared in the window. I hadn't even heard his truck pull in. I don't how it happened. How does anything like that happen? He had a thick, doughy cock that became as hard as a marble rolling pin. He went slowly at first, like a big boy in wooden shoes learning to waltz, but at the end I thought we both might go tumbling off the roof into the rose garden, his giant slab hands on my shoulders, me crying out when I came, a hundred white sailboats flecked across the blue lake beyond.

The shame and strangeness of it. The uncomfortable satisfaction.

I took a long hot bath after, and drank half a bottle of brandy, then slept for three hours. That night I fucked my girlfriend five times, ramming and reaming her until I thought the intensity of her orgasms might rupture her very being—a continuous explosion of ectoplasm and honey. "Christ!" she wheezed in the dark of early morning, "What got into you?"

Fortunately for the sake of my sanity and my academic standing, I had friends like Mark, a fellow graduate student and instructor, a Canadian who'd worked his way through UBC driving logging trucks. He had a deep radio-guru voice honed by Export A cigarettes, black coffee, and French fries bleeding catsup, which he could suddenly make appear out of his briefcase as if by magic. Mark liked beer and bourbon, I liked Scotch—and we both liked dope. He'd been married, but his wife, a speech therapist who once gave him great backrubs and brought him vodka tonics in the bathtub, got the itch for some Indian restaurant-gangster and took their little son and moved back to Vancouver.

Mark lived in the Central District and managed an apartment building full of black people. I think he might've been the only white person on that street. He seemed to feel no awkwardness in his position. I was there several times when things got awkward—like the night when the man everyone called Peebo tried to set his wife on fire, and Mark calmly talked him out of it. Or when all 275 pounds of Good Gal Lois would waddle down the concrete stairs and offer Mark a head job in return for some more slack on her rent (an offer which to my knowledge he always politely declined). Or all the visits warranted or uncalled-for by the Seattle Police. Mark took it all in stride and not only openly talked about what he was studying and reading, and how he made his living, but also taught remedial English at some community center in South Seattle—he'd actually recite Milton with great conviction.

This wasn't an audience predisposed to appreciating the English classics, but Mark never modified himself in any way to suit other people's expectations. It was difficult not to admire him, for he was always so very much himself. Single, lonely, living in this marginally acceptable cinderblock apartment, which he was given by virtue of his management position, driving back and forth to Vancouver to see his young son, coping with his ex-wife's flip-outs, grading term papers, and preparing lectures while people shot up heroin and yelled obscenities, then driving in the rain in his old Datsun to some blank municipal building to explain colloquial expressions to recently arrived speakers of Cantonese, all the while studying German to pass his Ph.D. language exam, finishing up his graduate classes, and chipping away at the outline of a monster dissertation—he did it all with a kind of crazy Miltonic lumberjack sense of mission and possibility.

The thought that that he'd never get a proper academic position at a decent university—and that he might be teaching Asians how to ask where the bathroom is for the rest of his working life—never occurred to him. He remains the only person I've ever known who could quote from memory "To His Coy Mistress" while eating deep-dish Mexicana pizza, and then jump effortlessly to discussing the starting lineup for the next Seattle Seahawks game.

One night after we'd smoked some dope, he led me to this rib joint down the street—some sort of Mississippi Delta mirage in the middle of black Seattle. We ordered what seemed like a fifty-five-gallon drum of fatback ribs smothered in smoky barbecue sauce and rolled it back to Mark's apartment, sat down like animals, and started gnawing and belching like animals. Then this neighborhood coke fiend named Tiny comes pounding on Mark's door with a Beretta, and Mark looks up, his eyes almost swollen shut, mouth full of pig meat, and says, "We're eating ribs, Tiny, come back later." I'll be damned if Tiny didn't go away and come back with two six-packs of Michelob, and we sat around picking at the bones, drinking beer, and watching Sabu in *The Elephant Boy* on TV.

Today, no one knows or cares what a good forklift driver I once was, or what a lousy janitor, or that I worked in the rail yards in Massachusetts, ripping through a pair of work gloves a day, slugging down the glassiest sledgehammer homemade vodka you've ever not tasted from a *Bionic Woman* plastic thermos with a group of mad Russians, who could fix absolutely anything—except their own questionable visa status, and so as engineers they were forced to work as laborers and factory hands. We ranted about Dostoyevsky, chess, and Kentucky Fried Chicken, huddled around drums of coal fires in the roundtable sheds where these demented young Irishmen from Revere would fight bare fisted, sweating like horses, while money changed hands and their blood splattered on the concrete. And after the fight, you could go out and break off an icicle and hit fungoes with snowballs into the dark, with the smell of steamed cabbage and diesel thick in the air.

Mark understood all this perfectly. He'd done time in logging camps and canneries. He'd lost a brother on an Alaskan fishing boat.

John understood too. His office was next to mine—a quiet eighteenth-century scholar who played the harpsichord and had a deaf child by an earlier marriage. Outside his teaching, he worked at a liquor store and had been robbed twice at gunpoint. Ramona, his girlfriend, was an outrageous Latina getting a degree in rhetoric and composition. She'd been a stand-up comic, run a taco stand outside Warner Bros., operated a mobile dog-washing service, worked for a bail bondsman and trained as a dental technician.

Such innocence then. Such inspired depravity. Roasting whole giraffes and setting off fireworks. Big, painterly fits of pasta and red wine. Pubic readings. All sorts of black silk stocking laudanum séances with Byron by candlelight.

But mainly they were days of hope and longing, of idealism and unexpected intimacies. To lie in bed after sex and discuss Roland Barthes. To sit on the rail of the Ferry Terminal with a newspaper of boiled prawns and thick lemon wedges and listen to a thirty-four-year-old woman with the breasts of an eighteen-year-old tell how she accidentally set fire to her house when she was six—and how her father chased her down the street with a hatchet when he found out.

I listened to many confessions and private theories then. And I read great books. I read *Moby Dick* in my canoe or lying on the boat dock on Lake Washington. The night I finished the novel by flashlight, under a full moon, I went up to the house, opened all the windows, and put on a tape of whale songs. I turned the stereo up as high as it would go, to hear those immense mammals singing with the moonlight flooding in. Until the neighbors called the cops. (Just as had happened to Jim Briggs way back in New Hampshire, and so saved him from hanging himself, as it turned out.)

I met Raymond Carver when he came to read. He wasn't a good reader, but he was very funny afterwards, when we went to a professor's house for a party. He was the only one who didn't drink. I had a long and involved conversation with poet-laureate-to-be Mark Strand over warm white wine. He complained about the absence of acceptable prosciutto in Salt Lake City, and with a straight face, proclaimed himself to be the city's most significant cultural attraction outside the Mormon Tabernacle Choir. And I smoked marijuana with Stanley Elkin in his motel room, both of us breaking out in spasms of weeping laughter. He'd come out from St. Louis for a writer's conference and I was his driver, assistant and dope connection. "I'm old enough to be your mother," he quipped. He told me about a fight he got into at a diner outside Chicago when he was just a squirt. Some guy called him "Ikey" and Stanley threw him across a table. He said it was the best moment in his life.

I never met Richard Hugo, who may have died unshaven for all I know. "What endures is what we have neglected," he wrote, although I feel as if I heard him say that in a bar—to me.

All these years later, I'm still wondering what it means, and what became of those lost colleagues and lovers of mine. All those breaths shared and lives not led. Those unsolved mysteries. Did Jane eventually kill herself? Or is she alive and sane—maybe even happy? Where's Mark teaching? Did he remarry? Whatever did happen to that squirrel?

FAITH AND LIGHTNING

When I was growing up, everyone was experimenting. Not just scientists and the military—the Garibaldis, the Crawfords, my parents. Formerly stable, circumspect people started literally blowing up their personal laboratories on a daily basis. At times it was reckless, sure. But there was also an innocence and an exuberance to it—and an insistence on finding out for oneself. "I know it may look like we're lazing away this lovely afternoon, but we're really experimenting with ginatonics." And it went on from there.

On an ordinary Wednesday night, my father might spontaneously drink a Rusty Nail or two, slip out the back door, and drive to the Elwood Theater for a late show of *Soldier in the Rain*, starring Steve McQueen, Jackie Gleason, and Tuesday Weld. And then pop into the International House of Pancakes for blueberry waffles on the way home.

My mother wore a beehive hairdo and talked about existentialism. She listened to Van Cliburn and Leontyne Price while painting her fingernails fire engine red (my father preferred Eddy Arnold and Hank Snow and, when he was preaching, experimented with having some of these country-western songs included in the choir's program).

You could go to Larry Blake's on Telegraph Avenue and overhear a man in a turtleneck sweater with a Van Dyke beard discussing Marxism in terms of Thousand Island dressing. There were rathskellers and coffeehouses. And big seafood restaurants. They served goldfish crackers in the clam chowder and had bad oil paintings of shipwrecks on the walls and a suave light-skinned black man with a bow tie at the piano, playing "Ebb Tide." Sometimes there was a pirate's treasure chest, where kids could take bamboo poles and "fish" for prizes. People today talk about "family restaurants" as if they were just invented. I remember when restaurants had high chairs *and* bongo drums and everyone made use of both. Happy Hour in the Outrigger Room never ended. Parents drank martinis, kids drank Shirley Temples, and everyone played games with straws in the ashtrays. Sometimes we'd go a different way home and almost get lost. Nowadays, I never have time to try a new route, and I hate getting lost. It's dangerous—when it's not frustrating.

My parents did a lot of dangerous things. Like entertaining. Sometimes we had luaus. My mother and sister would demonstrate the hula, Dad would perform with fire, and I'd smash coconuts with my junior geologist's hammer. Other times Mom would wear a snakeskin pantsuit. People talked about Edgar Cayce and Margaret Mead. And they experimented with cocktails: Screwdrivers, Harvey Wallbangers, Black Russians, and Pink Squirrels. A tray would go around with pigs-in-a-blanket, or Ritz crackers sprayed with Snack Mate cheddar cheese spread. Someone would put on Trini Lopez *Live at PJ's* or Sergio Mendes and the Brazil 66. Games were played—like passing a potato around under your chin.

Once, on her second mai tai, in the middle of a sentence that brought together Audrey Hepburn and Maslow's hierarchy of needs, my mother dropped a monkeypod bowl loaded with radishes and cherry tomatoes into a swimming pool and I had to dive for them (pretending to reenact the escape scene from *Captain Nemo and the Underwater City*). Then everyone started diving for them, clothes or not. What a game that was, particularly when there was nothing left to find. Later, I'd be told to get into my pajamas but I'd just fall asleep behind the couch, with the dog hair, the bobby pins, and the old Life Savers, and in the morning I'd find that I was in my bed. Magic. Every party an adventure.

My father got me driving before I could even reach the pedals—in traffic. After the third police warning, he'd take me in our blue Impala out to Golden Gate Fields and I'd herd seagulls around the puddles of rainwater in the vast empty parking lots—or at the School for the Deaf behind the Albany Bowl, where the pro was a hunchback and wore a bright magenta bowling shirt with his name stitched over his heart. STEVE . . . from Akron. It didn't seem like the right sort of name for a hunchback. But, boy, could he bowl—207 average, even though he'd quit the circuit. One Christmas, Dad gave me bowling lessons with Steve the hunchback. You see? Experimentation. Discovery. Risk.

It could be whiteout conditions on the top of the Gun Barrel at Heavenly Valley and my father couldn't have been happier. There he'd be, on his 240-centimeter wooden skis that looked like they'd come off the wall above a fireplace in some Canadian hunting lodge, yodeling for God's sake in case anyone as mad as he was would come swooping down the slope and wipe us out. And down we'd come, my mother singing, perhaps some Puccini—unless she was chastising my father for putting us all at risk. Sometimes, in really scary situations, where no one but the ski patrol had any business being (and only then to rescue fools like us), my mother could sing and criticize Dad all at once. It was some secret breathing technique she'd taught herself. My father would ski with me between his legs—mind over mogul, following the fall line, down out of the storm. "A blizzard? You call this a blizzard?"

When I turned five, my parents decided they'd run a summer camp. Neither had any experience running a camp. Neither had any capital. They had never dealt with big insurance policies, or the bulk-buying of powdered eggs and vats of peaches and blackberry jam. No matter. They rented an old Army Corps of Engineers Camp in Glen Alpine above Fallen Leaf Lake in Tahoe, from a man who was rumored to have been in prison once in Carson City. Dad hired a 300-pound woman from Turlock and her three daughters (feral girls she frequently spanked bare-assed with the flat of her giant butcher knife) to do the cooking. Then we spent two weeks sweeping and scrubbing out the rough timber cabins full of spiders and raccoon shit. Mom ran the music and drama programs; Dad ran the sports. They had twenty-eight paying kids from the Bay Area, one official staff member, and a local boy who'd been kicked in the head by a horse, to do the heavy lifting.

My mother and her students put on plays and scenes in little halls around Lake Tahoe and for the many other camps around Fallen Leaf. *The Winslow Boy*; *My 51st Dragon*; *Sorry, Wrong Number*; *Hoosier School Master* (which I always thought was a question).

Blazing aspen-leaf afternoons . . . the last light on the mountains, particularly Tallac, with its perpetual cross of snow, the light my father called Alpenglow. The chattering of kids in makeup and funny clothes—a big cardboard dragon tail. The old monster Chevy truck, which Dad bought in Truckee from a man missing three fingers, on the punishing dirt road down to Fallen Leaf Lodge for ice-cream sandwiches. Smell of maple syrup and sausages . . . the bear Dad blinded with his flashbulb.

The old man taught the older kids how to rock climb and fly-fish, while I caught ladybugs in the skunk cabbage and got the blacksmith to make me a horseshoe nail ring that turned my finger green. Every night, there'd be a performance around Fallen Leaf Lake or Lake Tahoe.

The highlight of the summer was a packhorse expedition into Desolation Valley, which wasn't swarming with backpackers then. The water was clean to drink. You could catch your limit of eastern brook trout in Lake Aloha and not meet another soul. You could sing around the campfire and watch shooting stars. Thinking you could count them.

It was quite a foray. Just my mother and father to supervise all those kids, including my ten-year-old sister, her "boyfriend" (who grew up to become a cowboy and a blacksmith), and five-year-old me. We got the horses from the Camp Richardson stable, but instead of a horse, my father was given a mule—eighteen and a half hands high, with a mean-looking, close-cropped mane, like a Marine haircut. The animal was so black it appeared to glisten, as if it was wet with oil. My father was beside himself because it reminded him of the mules they used during the war, when he was in the ski troops—the memory of which got him braying (my father did world-class animal imitations and was said to be able to capture subtle nuances like the difference in the moos of Holstein and Jersey cows). The giant mule, whose name was Floppy, took exception to the braying and it was all Dad could do to wrestle the creature back in line.

Perhaps this is why he didn't check the cinch on my horse's saddle. As soon as we were out of sight of the stables, my horse decided to make a break for it, eager to get back on the feedbag. The saddle slipped enough for me to lose the reins and suddenly I was on a big-barreled Arabian mare, swerving under low hanging pine branches, holding on for all I was worth. Shades of my sister's Shetland pony.

My mother shifted from singing songs from *The Music Man* to raving at my father, and he swung out from the front of the pack line and pounded around to cut us off—the mare so terrified of the massive black mule (which at full gallop was simply an awesome/gruesome spectacle of meat and muscle), she about burst her heart and took me clean over a split-rail fence that made me lose my Wheaties. Dad had never done any jumping either, but he drove the mule right at the rail without a hint of hesitation. Floppy cleared it like an Olympic hurdler going over a croquet wicket.

I was crying—I thought I'd pooped my pants. Dad got me back on another horse without a single word. I think he knew that if I had even half a chance I'd have been overcome by fear, and after my mother had had a fight with the cook for what she considered lewd behavior on the part of the daughters, she wasn't about to leave me back at camp. So there was no choice.

Two hours later, while stopped at the Floating Islands, a small lake filled with reedy hummocks that actually drift around, I fell through one and got totally soaked. Even in high summer the water was icy cold. I had to have all my clothes stripped off and to stand by a fire, naked, wrapped in a horse blanket while all the older kids laughed.

We lurched from near-disaster to disaster. Katy Wyman fell and hit her head. Of course, no one wore helmets in those days—that would've been too sensible. As we crossed the Rainbow Bridge, a narrow portion of trail not much wider than a packhorse, the fine line we were walking was made painfully clear. You could look down on your left and watch a thin stream of stones and sand triggered by the horses, tumbling what seemed like a hundred feet into the lake below. One misstep and that would've been it. If just one horse had kicked or nipped another right at that moment, we could all have gone over the precipice.

Then, coming into the valley from the north end, the weather changed, as it does quickly in the mountains. The sky went very dark, smelling of ozone and the greasy cinder chips of the shale. The horses grew tense and jumpy, straining at their bits and bucking, their hooves plinking on the riprap hard enough to strike sparks. Mad white-hot barbs of lightning started slashing the sky, thunder echoing back and forth behind the peaks like mortar fire. We were completely exposed. The air became supercharged with electricity, so that a glimmer of St. Elmo's fire seemed to ripple over the chain of horses. My father's mule was so black and wet looking now, it was like it was made of living obsidian, its huge corn-sheath ears with the scissor-pointed tips erect, nostrils dilated.

It seemed to take hours for us to negotiate the treacherous trail down off the ridge into the valley, hot rain spitting at us like a mist of gasoline. Everyone was silent, concentrating fiercely on the clip-clop stone stepping of the horses and the darkness bearing down on us. Except for my father. He was riding tail-end Charley and he started yodeling. The darker it got, the louder he wailed. Then my mother, who was out front on her Tennessee Walker, began to answer back in full Eastman School of Music soprano, their voices rising to meet each other in counterpoint to the thunder, ringing the line of us kids on down into the shelter of the valley.

The weather waited until we'd made camp and had the horses carefully tethered in the lee of a huge outcropping of granite boulders, then the god-crack opened and split the summer darkness firehead down. Shrapnel and hail. Storm giants drunk on waterspouts. It was unbelievable.

Dad had ruled against the two-man tents we carried and, with the help of the older boys, set up a single big lean-to with his trusty oil-smelling canvas lashed to the old circus tent spikes he carried just in case. He wisely figured that in smaller groups in separate tents, some of the kids could get pretty scared, especially if the storm raged all night—which it did—all of us huddled around Dad's mining lantern, singing songs, the sky so fiery bright with the lightning you could see X-rays of your hands in the air.

Two days later, when we got back to Glen Alpine, the kitchen staff mutinied for more money, then stole all the frozen chickens and the toilet paper and hit the road. My mother ended by hacking up a soggy corned beef in a kitchen frantic with bluebottles and yellow jackets, as the Turlock contingent, in a nasty parting gesture, had slashed all the window screens. I can see her now. She, who struggled to make oatmeal for a family of four, was now forced to make it for thirty-four. I'm certain she was on the verge of an emotional meltdown the entire last week, but her pride and her energy saw her through (although I came to believe that anyone making meatloaf should be licensed).

She wasn't going to let my father's misguided choice in personnel destroy her dream. It wasn't even going to slow her down. My parents finished the summer with buckets of rotting fish, two thousand moldy hot dog buns, and 250 gallons of sour milk. They paid too much for insurance, too much for the lease on the camp, too much for equipment rental, too much in utilities, too much in food, too much in wages. Too much. After the kids had all gone home, my father filled up one of the horse troughs and took a bath in baked beans. Why? Well, his answer was that he'd never had enough beans to do so before. This raised many questions in my young mind, and made me consider the possibility that my father had just lost his. My mother knew better, certain that this event had occurred long before.

It was a financial disaster that almost swamped the family, and yet in another column of figures, Jeff Murcott, who had epilepsy and was so shy he could barely talk, had played Huckleberry Finn in the "Don't You Know What a Feud Is?" scene in front of a capacity crowd at the Stanford Family Camp. Rachel Steinberger landed a sixteen-inch cutthroat on her own, and gutted it. Brian Rossi, my mother's favorite student, whose father had a heart defect and couldn't take him camping and fishing, climbed the front face of Pyramid with my father. Britt Macaskill, whose dad was soon to become a state senator and who had hardly ever even wiped his own butt, changed a flat tire on the green truck in the pouring rain in Emerald Bay and rewired the laundry hall of a campground in Tahoe City when the lights blew during a performance of *The Dust of the Road*. He never ended up going to Boalt Law School as his father had hoped. He went to San Francisco State to study theater lighting, and then on to the Yale Drama School, and then New York and Broadway.

As for me, one of the Turlock terrors showed me how girls pee (something a lot of grown men aren't clear on) and taught me how to throw a steak knife at a ponderosa pine from ten feet away and get it to stick. I saw two martens frolicking in the wildflowers by Lily Lake, and recited the entire "Midnight Ride of Paul Revere" by candlelight to a church group in Sawmill Cove.

Whenever I think about the mistakes my parents made, even the wreckage—the yelling, the guilt and recriminations, the strange cast of strangers, the dreadful business decisions, and all the money dramas and desperation, I think back to times like the summer at Glen Alpine. They weren't people to let things like weather conditions or economic realities dampen their spirits—or to stop them from causing their share of damage in pursuit of their dreams. In this I feel sad, for I wonder if I have taken fewer risks of certain kinds in my life, but for the wrong reasons. I wonder if outside my prodigious drug and alcohol intake and minor flirtations with the criminal life, I have mistaken having less faith for having more sense. That would be like me.

There's a photograph of my mother and father before they were married, on the flagstone steps of a mountain cabin in Estes Park, Colorado. It's the summer of 1949, the summer they climbed Long's Peak together—Dad's climbing skills still fresh from the Alps of Italy and the war. Mom looks like Merle Oberon (a point she'll remind me of on my fortieth birthday on a fog-shrouded ferry heading to the San Juan Islands). She's shining with inner light even though covered in trail dust. Dad wears a smile almost as outlandish as his feather-flourished Tivoli trout fisherman's hat. They're poised on the edge of a ridge, a great vista spreading out before them.

Without knowing it, they're looking toward the decade of the 1950s. Disneyland will open soon, celebrating the Century of Progress with personal jetpacks and backyard heliports. The Supreme Court will outlaw segregation in the schools, Faulkner and Hemingway will win Nobel Prizes, Rocky Marciano will retire undefeated, Grace Kelly will marry Prince Rainier, the Gold Coast will become Ghana, signaling the end of the British Empire, and a "police action" in Korea will go terribly wrong. But my parents are smiling, eager for what lies ahead, believing in possibility. Experimentation. Discovery.

Today my mother is in her eighties. She needs money and can no longer drive at night. She's still looking forward. Her younger sister keeled over in the kitchen doing late-night bookkeeping for her church and never woke up. Her estranged older brother died of colon cancer. Her second husband, my stepfather, sleeps most of the day, but my mother rolls on like a force of nature. It will take a fleet of trucks going full speed or some especially insidious pathology to slow her down. Old age alone won't be enough.

My father didn't fare so well. He died hypertensive, diabetic, florid, bloated, bewildered, incontinent, and probably impotent too. He and his third wife were living on charity in a subsidized aged-care housing complex connected with a Presbyterian Church, a denomination he had many reservations about. He was fifteen years younger than any of the other men in the facility, and forty years younger than a couple of the women. Dad and Wife III were able to live in that cinderblock and barren concrete sanctuary, built on old garbage marshland in San Leandro, surrounded by the decrepit and dying, by virtue of his tenuous job counseling and assisting the senior pastor of the church, a giant Nordic woman who wore his balls around her neck. And yet, despite the harrowing indignity, Dad's files, the only thing he left to me, suggest that even at the end of the world, he was marshaling his forces to make a comeback.

In the journal he left behind, which he started keeping after he did some sort of workshop in the mountains of Santa Cruz, there's a curious progression. It begins with headlines like "Psychic Jack Schwartz Talks about Photosynthesis." Then there's a series of entries about creating a Crystal Mantra. Then come the "dialogues," in which he personifies various issues in his life and has discussions with them, like the dialogue with his "Mystic Thinker" subpersonality, or some lost girlfriend from college days. This degenerates rather hilariously into the dialogue with a bank loan . . . "I am a person who tried to get a loan to buy a condominium and was turned down for not having a secure income."

ME: Why did you have to happen to me on top of everything else that has been coming down on me lately?

LOAN: You had carefully laid the groundwork for me happening long before I was even in the process of being considered.

ME: I suppose you are referring to my freelance way of working.

LOAN: Yes, and your eagerness to pay the lowest possible income tax. You don't really look too good on paper.

After this, the journal wanders through embarrassing erotic fantasies and a catalogue of fears about money and health, drinking, and so on. Then, at the end, in the months just before he died, it takes an unexpected turn. Dad was preaching occasionally again, which terrified him—he who had once been so calm and natural before a crowd. Much of the drinking at that late stage may simply have been some means of coping with the fear. But he kept facing it, and as the journal clearly shows, he was fighting his way back.

It must've been horrendous for him to reread old sermons like "The Roots and Fruits of an Enduring Marriage" (twice divorced, untold affairs) or "The Secret Formula for Success" (he'd taken to wearing robes when we went out because he could no longer fit into his old clothes and he didn't have enough money to buy a new wardrobe). But he reworked these old sermons, modifying and adapting them for the predominantly elderly congregation. And he'd started clipping snippets and articles—quotations and anecdotes that could supply him with ideas for new sermons. For instance, he'd saved a story on Roy Cleveland Sullivan, the so-called Spark Ranger of Shenandoah National Park, who was struck by lightning seven times and donated his lightning-burnt ranger hats to the Guinness World Record exhibit halls in New York City and Myrtle Beach.

The last few pages are devoted to Thor Heyerdahl, of all people, the Norwegian adventurer-anthropologist, most famous for the Kon-Tiki raft voyage across the Pacific, and the Ra expeditions in papyrus boats. The final entry is a page torn out of an old paperback version of the book *Kon-Tiki*—Heyerdahl's account of his invitation/plea to his old friend Torstein Raaby to accompany him.

> Am going to cross the Pacific on a wooden raft to support a theory that the South Sea Islands were peopled from Peru. Will you come? I guarantee nothing but a free trip to Peru and the South Sea Islands and back, and you will find a good use for your technical abilities on the voyage. Reply at once.

> Next day the following telegram arrived.
> "Coming. Torstein."

My father decisively circled the last line and placed beside it an exclamation mark. Then he repeated the phrase in his own hand . . . *Coming. Torstein.*

He was going to use this excerpt as the basis of a sermon. I think that he recognized in these two words a previously unexpressed motto for his own life. His creed.

When I think of him like that, I don't see the Old Crow and the landfill, and the urine stains. I don't think of him the way he died that night, on the floor of the little apartment with the paramedics trying to revive him. I see him as he was that day in Desolation Valley, astride the giant mule.

The sky is as black as the mule. The hairs on my arms and neck are anxious, like iron filings around a magnet. Thunder booms out between Dick's and Jack's Peaks. The kids' bodies are stiff with fear. And my father is yodeling. Coming down the steep, slick switchback, the air seems to be raving with static electricity and my father is yodeling. As if that will keep the lightning away.

And damn me if it didn't.

**TO END BEFORE YOUR TIME
IS WHERE ALL THE
TROUBLE GROWS**

HOME AWAY—RETURN TO CODA

Yes, whatever did happen to that squirrel?

Once, long ago, they told us in school there was a time when a squirrel could cross an entire state without ever touching the ground. But they didn't tell us that California foothills that had been golden for centuries would suddenly lose their live oaks and hawks to brick-veneer houses sprouting silver antennae that shone in the sun. Those houses filled the entire valley in less than two years and made us think even more intently about the squirrels of the not-so-distant past.

Then one night, when the moon was full and there were no good television shows on, the idea came to me—like a magical cure. Like the night I taught myself how to ride a bike.

Maybe we could turn the houses back into golden grass and trees, if we traveled the twenty-two miles of the valley without ever touching the ground—leaping over the shingles and ceramic tiles of all those roofs—at night when no one was watching and we were supposed to be in bed. We could reclaim the roofs. All of them. If we started from Noel's house, in the newer subdivision, we stood a chance.

There were three of us in on the expedition—Noel, Kim and me. Kim thought we should tell the newspapers or the Guinness Book of World Records, but Noel and I wanted to keep the journey a secret.

We wanted to leave while the moon was bright. We wanted to leap between the black-windowed houses with the dogs barking and the water gleaming in the swimming pools.

It was harder work than we thought. Kim was fat and sometimes almost fell. We heard sirens and got scared, but the air was sweet and biting with the scent of distant alfalfa and freshly watered lawns. We could hear the steady whoosh of the trucks on the interstate as we always could back in our beds, but the sound was more acute and resonant in the open air and made us wonder harder than ever where they all were going.

We kicked sun-dried, pulpy newspapers out of rain gutters, we whistled down chimneys, we broke off a TV aerial and carried it like a standard, then chucked it like a javelin into an empty doghouse. We were simultaneously explorers and burglars—two very great things to be at least once in life, and no one in the world knew where we were or why we'd gone.

We learned an important lesson that night. We found out you can hide behind a chimney while a dachshund barks its head off only so long before you realize it's a dachshund. You can cross a hundred roofs but you will never experience that delicious life-mad fear the same way again. You will never whisper as you whispered that first time, or feel so intimately concerned with the fine fur on a cat's back, seen in the sudden illumination of a flashlight held in a frightened homeowner's hand.

Twenty-two miles is a hell of a long way, and no, we didn't make it all the way, by any stretch of even our own imaginations. But did we return home? That's my question. Home is a mysterious place—seemingly the same but forever changed, when you've traveled as far as we did that night. So many years later, and I've lived a hundred lifetimes' worth of nights beneath that moon. I've scaled derelict oil tanks on a beach in North Africa, and fallen off a camel drunk in the heart of Australia, only to be awakened by wild horses splashing in a red-rock creek. Still I don't know if I found my way back home that morning or if I just reached a jumping-off place. Jump with me, go higher and higher.

I suppose the truth is, we leap from house to house, and inevitably sometimes we stay too long. We grow afraid. The distance seems too great. Eventually we forget how we arrived—we're so busy remaining.

If you ever get that way, my recommendation is to go up on the nearest roof. That's where the adventures begin. Have an expedition party—I may even join you. But we must leave immediately, because we have many roofs to cross and darknesses to leap before we learn the secret of returning.